GOD BEFORE BREAKFAST

Thoughts for the Day

Angela Tilby

SPCK

D0232379

For Anthony Phillips,
who introduced me to the book of Job
and encouraged me to consider a career in broadcasting,
with grateful affection

First published in Great Britain in 2005

Society for Promoting Christian Knowledge
36 Causton Street
London SW1P 4ST

Copyright © Angela Tilby 2005

All rights reserved. No part of this book may be reproduced or transmitted
in any form or by any means, electronic or mechanical, including
photocopying, recording, or by any information storage and retrieval
system, without permission in writing from the publisher.

SPCK does not necessarily endorse the individual views
contained in its publications.

British Library Cataloguing-in-Publication Data
A catalogue record for this book is available from the British Library

MORAY COUNCIL
LIBRARIES &
INFO.SERVICES

20 15 39 91

Askews

242

Typeset by Kenneth Burnley, Wirral, Cheshire
Printed in Great Britain by Ashford Colour Press

Contents

Contents

Contents

Foreword

The 'Thoughts' of My Friend Angela

I met Angela many decades ago while making a TV programme for the BBC at the Dominican Centre in Staffordshire. It was a genial, comfy place which didn't put on the religious style or go in for 'role models' and other ecclesiastical camp. It was built, as I remember, on top of a coal mine and the ground was liable to open at your feet as in *Don Giovanni*, which made us all thoughtful.

Angela didn't put on the style or play role models either; despite her theological learning. She was (and is) direct, open and, though traditional, not afraid of doubt. She didn't preach at you, she spoke to you. So we had deep discussions at the Dominican bar and in motorway 'eateries'– if that is what one can call them. Anyway, I took to her. She was the 'real thing', to use the pop jargon of those days, and we became friends. I was pleased for her and her Church when she and other women like her got ordained.

We haven't met much face to face in recent years. Life has pulled us in different ways. But we keep in touch thanks to the radio, TV and the *Today* programme. When she is on, I turn the volume up and don't turn over. Why? Because she examines the news of this world spiritually, uniting the earthly and the heavenly. Because she is not afraid of being honest and direct about 'hot' issues, whether moral or political.

Because she unites my breakfast paper with my inner life. Because the endings of her 'Thoughts' disconcert me and I ponder them during the day. Because she doesn't pretend she knows what God has for breakfast. So I trust her. I've learned a lot about people ranging from George Herbert to General Pinochet to Ms Lewinsky and to our Royal Family – fascinating.

This collection is good, user-friendly spiritual reading. I prescribe one of her 'Thoughts' a day with your first cup of coffee if, like me, you want help in glimpsing the Divine beneath the surface of trendy fashions and populist feelings. Thanks, Angela!

Lionel Blue

Introduction

Ever since I can remember there has been a religious slot on the *Today* programme before the 8 o'clock news. These few moments of uplift used to be the spiritual counterpart of *Keep Fit*, with Eileen Fowler. Both were designed to get you up and off to work in a positive frame of mind. At one point, the morning God slot was called 'Ten to Eight'. 'Thought for the Day' is its successor. (The Home Service and Radio 4 seemed to specialize in these rather apologetic titles, unlike the more robust and devotional *Lift Up Your Hearts* of the Light Programme and Radio 2!)

For some years, in my early twenties I actually produced 'Thought for the Day'. This was in 1974 when I was an enthusiastic, if inexperienced, radio producer with the BBC's Religious Programmes Department. It was recorded in batches on reel-to-reel tape and sent off in carefully labelled boxes to the library of current recordings. From there the right tape for the day would be fished out by the *Today* studio managers. The 'Thoughts' I produced were nearly five minutes long and used to begin with a little phrase of classical music, artfully faded under the opening words. The music was intended to be a buffer between the news and the reflection to follow which did not have to be particularly topical or of the moment. I worked with Lionel Blue, Eric James, Richard Harries and Austen Williams, the long-serving vicar of St Martin-in-the-Fields. I learnt a lot from these and other contributors about writing for the ear, about addressing an audience with complex attitudes to religion, and of responding at short notice to an unforeseen development in the studio or in the items leading up to the broadcast. 'Thought' was regarded as something of a flagship programme and was heavily monitored (and often sharply criticized) by the powers that be.

Then 'Thought' went live and immediately became a very different kind of animal. It now had to be topical and relevant. There was the possibility of interaction with the presenters;

the contributor had to learn to be much sharper and journalistically aware. As *Today* itself became more combative in tone, 'Thought' had to find a more prophetic edge, without falling into the trap of being party political. For years after my time as a radio producer my contact with 'Thought' was as a listener (I had left steam radio for television and was working as a documentary producer for *Everyman* and *Horizon*). Over breakfast I went through the gamut of reactions to 'Thought' depending on the content and tone that morning; irritation when a contributor seemed inadequate for the topic they had taken on, admiration on the occasions when they got it right, and puzzlement that what was inevitably of patchy quality was tolerated in what had become a hard-headed news-orientated environment. Then in 1994 I moved with the BBC's Religious Department to Manchester and found myself sharing office space with colleagues from radio. Greatly to my surprise, I was invited to contribute to 'Thought' myself and have been doing so ever since. I owe much to the friendly professionalism of David Coomes, Christine Morgan and the producers who comprise the 'Thought' team.

Contributing to 'Thought' is a privilege. It has taught me to dig deep from the Christian spiritual tradition to try to offer a response to the events of the day. Neither I nor the other contributors are asked to take part because we are experts on politics or have special solutions to the world's problems. 'Thought' is about trying to see an issue in the light of eternity and with the resources of wisdom beyond this world. I take it seriously, but not too seriously. Pomposity makes religion risible. A sense of eternity is all about regaining perspective, and not getting too hysterical at the dramas of the present moment. But in respect for the tradition of fasting before a trial, I don't eat anything before doing 'Thought', hence *God Before Breakfast*.

PRIEST AND COURTIER

26 February 1996

This is a week to remember George Herbert, the priest and poet, who died in 1633. At school assemblies we often bawled out his words: 'Let all the world in every corner sing, My God and King!' And, especially on Monday mornings, we'd go: 'Seven whole days, not one in seven, I will praise thee.'

Most people think of Herbert as a gentle country clergyman who wrote of flowers and prayer and church bells, Easter and divine love. 'Love bade me welcome, yet my soul drew back, Guiltie of dust and sinne . . .' It's less well known that Herbert was once an ambitious young MP in an age of conflict and unrest which ended in civil war. He did well out of a corrupt system of patronage and got himself a life's income as a royal favour.

If the politics of his day were in turmoil, the Church was also in a mess. Run by the seriously rich and not always for the benefit of the poor, it was divided between hard-faced Bible bashers and high churchmen. There was much controversy about the size of pulpits and whether clergy should wear black gowns or white surplices.

Herbert's poetry came from the conflict between his ambition and his God. There was something in his soul that the high-profile life didn't satisfy. When his royal patron died he was dropped from court circles, and that was when he found his way towards ordination. He became Rector of Bemerton in Wiltshire at the age of 37. He turned out to be a good priest. People found him conscientious, energetic and humble. And they could understand him. No pomp. No weasel words. 'Teach me, my God and King, in all things thee to see, and what I do in anything, to do it as for thee.'

As I think about Herbert's life I realize that I have only a vague notion about the day-to-day issues of his time. Monarch and Parliament, Church and State. Wars in Europe. The first pilgrims departing for the New World. But I can read his hymns and poems and they speak as freshly as they ever did. I think one reason is that Herbert never forgot that even the biggest affairs of the day are judged by eternity. After his briefly glittering career he chose to live and pray and die among poor farm labourers. Perhaps he realized that the small decisions of the human soul produced big consequences for them just as they did – and do – for those who legislate for the nation in Parliament.

His words from *The Church Porch* certainly have a fresh meaning on a morning when our national vices and virtues are up for debate in Parliament: 'O England, full of sin, but most of sloth, Spit out thy phlegm and fill thy breast with glory.'

PRIVATE VICE AND PUBLIC OFFICE

11 March 1996

There's an argument going on at the moment about whether private virtue is a necessary qualification for the holding of public office. Lots of people seem to think it is. The higher the office, the more we worry about whether the holder is morally up to it. What's behind this is an assumption that there should be a seamless continuity between what a person represents and his or her inner life. This isn't only true of the virtuous; sinners, too, must be consistent. If monarchs and ministers are required to be good, entertainers and celebrities must titillate us by having appropriately steamy private lives. No one can quite believe in Cliff Richard's portrayal of Heathcliff, because the inner Cliff is too pure for the part.

I think our judgements of character are in danger of becoming superficial. We've fallen into the trap of believing that transparency is a virtue. We're seduced by the appearances of things. Yet, 'Man looks on the outer appearance, but the Lord looks on the heart'. Those words of wisdom came to the prophet Samuel when he was trying to choose a king of Israel. They're words that still resonate.

Yesterday at the 8 a.m. Communion Service I read one of St Paul's stern admonitions against fornication, uncleanness, adultery, covetousness, foolish talking and whoremongering – on account of which cometh the wrath of God – to a rather quiet and respectable-looking congregation. I felt a bit embarrassed about it, relieved that the sheer rudeness of the text was varnished over by the decent obscurity of seventeenth-century English. Afterwards I found myself wondering why the compilers of the Book of Common Prayer wanted to alarm the faithful by banging on in church about the dangers of private sin. Perhaps they knew what we have forgotten – that in matters of passion, goodness is not always what it appears to be. Virtuous people are all sinners, and sinners never lose the chance to repent. You don't know what goes on behind the bowed head and praying hands, nor is it your business.

I am becoming rather nervous of those who have never put a foot wrong, never made an emotional fool of themselves, never done anything to regret. Such people are so scarily in control of their lives that I dread what they might do if they had any control over the rest of us.

Surely what matters in people who hold public office is that they accept and promote the value of what they represent, whether or not they are personally worthy. A gap between the ideal they uphold and the real lives they live is not insincerity but sanity, not hubris but humility.

TAKE . . . READ

13 May 1996

Sixteen hundred years ago in a garden in Milan a young man from north Africa became a Christian believer. He had been searching for *something* for many years and had tried quite a few of the spiritual disciplines and therapies on offer. He had a girlfriend he had abandoned – and a little son. He also had a ferocious mother who got at him for his fecklessness. He managed to find a good job in a university, but his underlying depression weighed him down. As he sat in the garden with tears in his eyes he heard the sing-song voice of a child next door, repeating the Latin words, '*Tolle, lege* . . .' 'Take, read'. In the end he took hold of a copy of the scriptures and read: 'Arm yourself with the Lord Jesus Christ, and spend no more thought on nature and nature's appetites.'

That conversion was a turning point in history, for the young man was Augustine, who became one of the greatest philosophers of the Western world.

I'm thinking of that summer garden because this time of year reminds me of the weeks I spent in the garden years ago trying to revise for exams. Bird song, cherry and magnolia blossom bring back a tremor of fear. Yet gardens in May were the places I learnt to learn. You see, I wasn't very attentive in class, but on my own, with a text, I would suddenly get the point.

Take, read. I think I must have been taught to read with the phonic system because I remember following the letters along a line with my finger, mouthing the sound until the sound suddenly gripped the letters of the page and I could make sense of what was before my eyes. At the age of three this was a miracle. It opened a whole world. It meant that at seventeen my mind was trained to cope with the academic trials that led to adulthood. I was able to learn, not through a teacher, but directly through a text.

4

Without books, without reading, our understanding is uninformed, our judgements narrow. We are open to manipulation by those who would steal our freedom. I suspect that the neglect of reading has to do with a wider kind of spiritual thuggery that is tearing us apart, and robbing us of belief both in God and ourselves. I sometimes think God would rather we were literate than that we were indiscriminately caring. Augustine found his true self through a child's cry and a challenging text. He met the living God on the page of a book, and it broke his heart and set him free. We must not deny our own children what God desires for them.

SCHOOL PRAYERS

16 July 1996

Hands together, eyes closed: 'Our Father, which art in heaven . . .' We had prayers twice in the school day when I was growing up in the 1950s. There was no doubt in my five-year-old mind that prayer was talking to God, someone bigger than the very large headmistress in her black dress, high heels and seamed stockings who led our daily rites. She was so fierce and frightening that I was impressed that she talked to God with deference. It gave me hope.

Prayers at my next school were called assembly, and happened once a day, in a bright, sunny hall. We sang a hymn, heard a Bible reading and were played in and out on the piano to 'Für Elise'. Prayers were taken by a rather gentle head teacher in a bluebell-coloured suit, who addressed the Almighty with weary familiarity. At my next, grown-up school, the arrangements were rather complicated. There were Jewish prayers and Catholic prayers and prayers to which everyone else went, except during exams when all prayers happened in the gym. By this time it was the 1960s. I was in my teens and prayers had become embarrassing. Solemn agnostic rows of sixth-formers stood with eyes unblinkingly open, sullenly examining their illegal nail varnish. Prayers by this time had taken on a rather Pelagian tone, so as to be relevant to unbelievers. Care was taken to avoid the squeamish bits about judgement and hell, and the more militant hymns, even though they were more fun to sing. There was much exhortation and stirring of social guilt, 'Make us more loving, caring, responsible . . .' Gone was the awesome strangeness of the God of my childhood, who might one day take my side against the adult world.

School Prayers are a contentious issue. What was originally undertaken as an acknowledgement of the transcendent is now justified because it gets the day off to a good start and produces a worthy moral tone. It does what those exercises and company songs do in big Japanese corporations, reminding you to work hard and do as you're told. My childhood memory rebels against all this. The God we prayed to then was different from us, different from the headmistress, different from our parents, different from the school. We addressed him in a different language, we shut our eyes and put our hands together. That was an acknowledgement of the sacred.

When the pupils returned to St Luke's Primary School in Wolverhampton yesterday after the tragic shooting, the headmistress led them in a hymn of praise to God, not denying their recent trauma, but reassuring them of a strength and comfort beyond what fallible adults can ever hope to provide.

A TIME TO BE BORN AND A TIME TO DIE

25 March 1997

The young coma victim, Miss D, has gone home to her family. Her doctors believe it is in her best interests that she should be allowed to die. She has no awareness, no sense of self. Her case is complicated by the fact that her body is still producing reflexes. But as far as we can tell, the person Miss D *was* is suspended in a living death. It doesn't take much imagination to realize that her family and friends are also in her living death, unable to mourn her passing, unable to move on. She has no relationships any more with those who love her. Nor is her spirit free to find itself in God since she is hindered by what the Book of Common Prayer calls 'the burden of the flesh'. Still, it's a terrible thing for her family to have to watch her fading away. There are anxious questions. How do we know that she knows nothing? How can we be sure that she will not suffer? And the answer is, we don't ultimately know – we can only take the best advice available, and then in fear and trembling make the hard and heartbreaking decision.

Of course people have rushed to condemn the judgement. There has been talk of 'barbaric practices' and 'torture' as if what has been happening were not a form of torture. All who care for Miss D must fear that somehow there lurks some shadow of awareness, even sensations of terror and pain. Just to think of her condition is to sense disquiet.

But that doesn't necessarily make it right to overthrow the decision of the family and the doctors and the judge. They have had to contend with life and death, enduring their share of moral agony. I think it is infantile to believe that there is a trouble-free solution to Miss D's case; that we can come out of it with spotless consciences.

What has been missing so far is any sense of the mercy of God. We can't always know we've got it right, but I think God invites us to be bold rather than fearful. I find it consoling that so many of the saints are shockingly casual about death, seeing it not as a tragedy, but a release into eternal joy. The veil between this world and the next is a thin one, but heaven requires that people really die, not linger, frozen in time. Try as I might, I cannot see that Christianity ascribes an *absolute* value to human life on earth. It is an atheistic ploy to make a fetish of the body, to divinize biological life at the expense of the Spirit. There is a time to be born and a time to die. A good death is a fruitful death – as the creeds of Christendom insist – when they speak of that other agonizing death on a cross, endured for the living and the dead, for us men and for our salvation.

UNEMPLOYMENT

9 April 1997

It's blue, green and yellow with red titles. Yesterday's multi-coloured report by the churches argues that all the political parties are ignoring *unemployment*. Of course, the parties have responded, 'No, we're not!' So, has the report just fizzed – a holy cocktail of demands and admonitions – only to disappear within hours of publication? I hope not, because I think the report's value is in the small print; the footnotes, the *principles* rather than the *policies*.

The churches would be betraying the Bible and two thousand years of teaching if they did not repeat the basic principle of relieving poverty. There's really no arguing with that. But policies are more difficult. We all have to make an intelligent judgement about which set of policies will actually deliver what our principles require. This is where the churches' position becomes delicate. Supposing no political party is offering policies which can meet Christian principles? You could argue back that democracy requires that principles have supporters. If they don't, it's likely that they're either unworkable or wrong, and then the scene is set for a typical battle. The churches are on one side, apparently with all the principles, but all they can actually do is to condemn a cowardly, complacent set of politicians, and, implicitly, a cowardly, complacent electorate.

And that's where I come back to the small print. We've known for years that the world of work was changing. I remember futuristic documentaries showing paperless offices and robot-built cars, silicon chips raining from heaven. The pundits told us that the age of the work ethic was over. There would be no more permanent work but a wonderful mixture of work and leisure for everyone. No one prepared us for what actually happened. No one told us that we would end up with a creative, nervous, driven, enterprising, stressed-out society of people at work, alongside a hard ring of people who are also stressed out and nervous, but because they're excluded from work.

Somehow both halves are losing out. The churches have described in painful detail what it means to lose out through poverty. But perhaps they're less comfortable describing what's happening to the so-called well-off. They see complacency. But I also see massive fear, guilt and insecurity about the future. The Bible envisages a rhythm of work and rest, effort and recreation. And this is where the sin of our time really bites into our being, for none of us knows how to live this rhythm any more. We're either dying to get work – any of it – or dying from work, too much of it. So we come to the paradox, that the rich and the poor both need some of what the other has. There's no complacency in admitting what you need – and acting on it.

GOING BACK TO SCHOOL

5 September 1997

Most of the rebellions I remember from my schooldays were acts of high-spirited naughtiness, which were either tolerated or punished according to how much they disrupted the life of the community. My refusal to sing the part of a crocus in the school pageant was treated kindly – I was a shy little thing after all. But blowing soap bubbles in assembly was judged a serious offence meriting discipline. Teachers and heads knew where the boundary lay between order and disorder, and so when to be kind and when to be tough.

These days it seems much less easy to know where those boundaries lie. Take the story of Sarah Briggs. She was expelled from her school in Mansfield for reporting to a local newspaper that too many staff were staying away and that her education was being disrupted. But the school took her complaint as rebellion and threw her out. Last month, after a public campaign, she was reinstated. But yesterday, on the first day of a new term at Sarah's school *the teachers* protested – over a timetable which they said was unworkable.

Perhaps it is not surprising that there is a desperate shortage of school heads and deputy heads and that teachers themselves are in short supply. These jobs are just too hard, too demoralizing.

A prayer being used this week in the Church's daily services asks God to govern the hearts and minds of those in authority – and to bring the families of the nations into subjection to the just and gentle rule of Christ. That prayer makes me realize how hopeless it is trying to keep order without a transcendent *something* to which *all* are subject. Even if you don't believe in God, you have to have some template of justice and gentleness moulding your actions if you are to embody those qualities to others.

The problem is that, without God – without what God stands for – we all become delinquents, lost children looking for someone to draw the boundaries for us and pat us on the back when we do well. The depression and anxiety among teachers and heads is only part of a wider loss of boundaries in society. Unwilling to take responsibility we all look for scapegoats. Parents compete with their children for their own time and attention. No one wants to be head. No one wants to be boss. And in that vacuum of vocation there is a danger that those who still are attracted to the job are drawn more by the thrill of power than by the creativity of service. Yet between tyranny and anarchy is that haunting notion of 'the just and gentle rule of Christ'. Which would you choose for your children, or for yourself?

RUSSIAN CHURCH AND STATE

11 September 1997

Moscow has been celebrating its 850th anniversary this month. There's been a renaissance of art and architecture. The Cathedral of Christ the Saviour has risen from the ruins of the past – a visible symbol of holy Russia. Yet there's an uneasy side to all this triumph. There *is* religious freedom in the new Russia, but some faiths are freer than others. New legislation is about to boost the privileges of Russian Orthodox Christians by once again curtailing the rights of other religions. Why is there this hard, even brutal streak in what should be a rebirth?

In the dark days of the Iron Curtain I fell in love with Eastern Orthodoxy. The candles and glittering icons spoke to me of a mystical kind of Christianity that I had never met before. It was evoked for us all recently in that prayer of John Tavener to the angels which ended the funeral of Princess Diana. But in spite of its other-worldliness, Orthodoxy has a curious tendency to sanctify the rulers and authorities of this world. I never quite understood why Eastern Christianity had such an investment in power until two years ago when I bought a Russian icon in the Holy Land. It had twelve exquisitely painted scenes. Eleven of them were familiar incidents in the life of Christ, but the twelfth was rather different. It showed the first Christian emperor, Constantine and his mother Helena, staring out in stiff brocaded vestments. They had haloes. They were saints. The message of the twelfth scene was clear: the kingdom of this world has become the kingdom of our Lord and of his Christ. State and Church are one.

This is a potentially dangerous message. If the State and the Church are the same thing, how can the Church ever criticize the State? It was an agonizing problem for Russian Christians under Communism. Here was a godless state where survival had to be bought with silence. But now the tide has turned in the Church's favour, and the temptation is to forget the purging pain of those seventy years and make a crusade of Russian nationalism. There's even a move afoot to declare Nicholas II, the last of the Tsars, a saint.

Christian faith lives best when it lives by imagination. It is in covenant with the future, it takes its energy from a heartfelt dissatisfaction with the injustice of our fallen world. Jesus once compared his disciples to the salt of the earth; they were to impart a sharp taste to our everyday life, a tang of the kingdom of freedom to come.

His question could still be asked of the Russian Church: *if salt has lost its savour, how will you season it?*

SCRAP HEAP

19 September 1997

I've been moving house this week so I've been spending time at the council refuse tip, abandoning things that should have been thrown out years ago. A warped guitar, a broken food processor, thick with sinister, treacly dust; sad, bagged jumpers. I have to confess to a secret pleasure in my solitary visits to refuse tips. I like the way the cars pile in, the boots fly open, the black sacks are dragged to the nearest compacter, and then the liberating moment when the stuff is thrown in! You go on your way, unburdened.

It's something to do with accepting the fact of waste and the work of time. Nature is prodigal – like us – and inefficient. Bits of waste can feed bits of life, garbage bags are scavenged, parts of cars and stereos can be welded into different bodies. But there's always a residue, a useless bit that no one wants. The tidy part of us rejects the messiness of nature, and our own messiness. We've lost a sense of the recklessness of creation, and how its abundance always exacts a price; death, slime, ash and decay. Yet, in Christian faith, waste and death are the very hinge of creation. We fear them, but we're grateful for them too. 'We glory in thy cross, O Lord', our liturgy says, 'And we praise and glorify thy holy resurrection'. A wasteful, squalid death opens the door to life and hope.

I felt a huge sense of relief when we heard recently that much of the effort to recycle household waste was useless. It costs more in energy than it saves. It worries me that we put so much emphasis on preserving and conserving. The terrible truth is that we can't hold up the cosmic clock any more than we can reverse the flow of time. Woolly mammoths are over and so are dinosaurs, and it's only in nightmares that they come back to haunt us. Fantasies where time is frozen or reversed and what is dead reproduces only itself, not something new. It is because nature is so random and variegated that it can produce the unexpected.

But to have hope in the renewal of life you have to lose your fear of time.

The removal van turned up at my new home and I wanted to weep for the loss of one life, and for the long effort that will fuel the start of another. In the light of eternity my domestic changes will seem pretty small stuff. But *in* the light of eternity, the universe itself is insubstantial and doomed for the scrap heap. The loveliness, the beauty, the giftedness behind it all – that is what remains and abides, ever ancient and ever new.

PARENTS AND CHILDREN

25 September 1997

Jack Straw's proposal that parents should pay for the wrongs of their children reminds me of one of the great moral debates of the Old Testament. On one side is the argument that sin breeds more sin. 'The iniquities of the fathers shall be visited upon the children to the third and fourth generation.' This is true, of course. The crimes of one generation have consequences forty, sixty, perhaps a hundred years later. Yet that observation is at odds with the opposite argument, that each generation starts with a clean slate.

When the Jews were exiled in Babylon, there was a lot of complaint that the young were being made to suffer for the sins of their forebears. There was a bitter little proverb going the rounds, 'The fathers ate sour grapes but it's the children's teeth that have been set on edge.' It was all so unfair. The prophet Ezekiel agreed, and announced that God had changed his strategy, and that from now on, each generation would be responsible for its own sins. He has God saying, 'Behold, all souls are mine. As the soul of the father is mine, so also is the soul of the son. The son shall not bear the iniquity of the father, neither shall the father bear the iniquity of the son.'

I'm glad the Bible had this argument with itself, because it helps us with our dilemma. All parents fail their children. All children carry that failure with them. But the way children turn out is not just the consequence of how they were brought up. Children are more than repositories for the sins of their parents. 'All souls are mine. The soul of the parent and the soul of the child.' We know there are children brought up well who turn out badly, and badly brought up children who make good, sometimes against terrible odds. There *is* a moral carry-over from generation to generation, but the results aren't always what one expects. Sin is sometimes re-inforced, but it's also sometimes redeemed. Many of the most generous and creative people have had ghastly childhoods.

The Bible knows we're up against it morally. Being good is not easy. We need all the help we can get. Parents, religion, schools, the police; TV stars and football heroes are all responsible for our children's values. But the parents' role is perhaps the greatest because their influence lasts the longest. It is right that they should be brought back into the picture, and asked to search their hearts when things go wrong. After all, redemption is a kind of buying back of the past, a chance to set right what is done amiss, in the hope that it is never too late for parents and children to save each others' souls.

THE RED HUNTER AND
THE PALE GIRL

28 November 1997

A red-faced hypertensive with a horse between his knees. A pale girl in leggings, weeping for a fox's death. Sometimes in a debate it's worth exploring the stereotypes simply because they tell us something even more important than the issue at stake, something of ourselves and God.

Yesterday I fleshed out the red-faced man and the pale girl in my mind as though I was their vicar. I decided that neither were regular churchgoers but that they both might turn up for a carol service or a funeral. I imagined them arriving at the church – the hunter first. He comes in to worship aware of the violence of nature. Animals feed off animals, there is blood and bone in the soil. He is a realist about death. He eats well and drinks well and hopes to die in his boots. For him nature has a rough kind of beauty which he feels part of. Hunting is a bond between man and horse and dog against a cunning predator. In the church he sees plenty of evidence of order keeping chaos at bay. Wooden pews, cut from trees and carved, the devil cast out as a screeching gargoyle spouting rain, the stern angels. He sees the rood screen and the crucified Lord with blood streaming from his side. He knows that there's a symmetry in things and that even when God comes down to earth he is hunted, killed and eaten, body and blood.

And then the pale girl. She comes into the church to rest in its silence. For her it is a great space enclosing a mystery. She sees the winged angels on the roof, the pale faces ringed with gold. She senses beyond and above the stone and the windows a transcendent peace which enfolds everything. This for her is God, beyond, within, nameless and uncontainable. She gazes at the thin saints, their bodies controlled by fasting; their temper calmed by the steady, daily discipline of refusal to do violence.

They do not kill or carry arms or ride or hunt. She senses that they weep at the waste of killing. She knows that everything is connected. A divine thread binds her to the whole of creation. She is glad that this house of God gives shelter to the lichens and the bats and the spiders. She sees the lion and the lamb lying down together, the Christmas beasts gathered quietly round the manger, the resurrected Lord bringing salvation to his persecutors.

What I realize now is that the Church holds two visions, neither of which can ever quite win. The red hunter and pale girl are keeping alive for us questions that are fundamentally religious. Are we indeed angels or animals? God's roughest beasts or messengers of his cosmic peace?

CANDLE OF HOPE

12 December 1997

Yesterday was the end of term at the theological college where I teach in Cambridge. We all sat on each side of our small chapel exhausted after ten hard weeks of intensive slog. Together we listened to the scriptures, and to poems and carols, and sang hymns for the season of Advent. Through the middle of us stood a line of candles. As the service progressed they were lit one by one, each from the light of the one before, so that points of light advanced down the chapel until the seventh candle was lit in front of the altar. And then I read the words of the risen Jesus from the Apocalypse, the last book of the Bible. 'I am the root and offspring of David, the bright morning star.' Advent prepares for Christmas, the coming of Christ. But it also warns of the end of all things, divine judgement and the winding up of history.

As I watched the candles flickering I thought of the Kyoto summit and its small achievement on greenhouse gases. I saw in my mind's eye the exhausted delegates, sleepless and bleary eyed, stumbling out with far, far less than many had hoped for.

Advent is a season of yearning, when the Church takes up the crying of all nations, all peoples, for justice, renewal and the hope of heaven. It's a dream that the wise King of the ages will come and set us free from the mess we've made of things. In the chapel yesterday I realized that the planet's sickness has brought us to a unique moment. Judgement is here and now. Never before in the history of the human race have all the nations and peoples of earth confronted exactly the same threat. Even in the age of the Cold War it was conceivable that one block of nations could actually win and the other lose. But at Kyoto we faced the possibility that we would all be either winners or losers. There are no enemies other than ourselves. It is a time of extraordinary opportunity. And yet so little was apparently achieved.

I think it would be wrong to be too depressed about the outcome of Kyoto. Even a small agreement is a moral and practical recognition that our world is one. It was a candle of hope being lit, and the next will be lit from it, as science and industry take up the challenge to work our planet less wastefully. And the next candle will come when we really want our world to be as beautiful to live in as we have seen that it is, rising silver and blue in dark space. The judgement that hovers over us could also be the moment of salvation – the moment when we see our world as though through the eyes of God.

MARTIN LUTHER KING

6 April 1998

It's thirty years since Martin Luther King was gunned down while supporting a workers' strike in Memphis, Tennessee. The anniversary has been tarnished by a row about who really killed him. It's claimed that his assassin was not James Earle Ray, who was convicted of the crime and is now serving life in jail. Instead King was the victim of a conspiracy involving the FBI, the Mafia, and the Intelligence Services. Apparently they were all out to get him for his leadership of the Civil Rights movement – and they did.

Conspiracy theories like this need to be investigated of course, but I think they often come from our sense of drama, the need to make a great death glamorous. I suppose it's oddly comforting to think that it wasn't a crazy inadequate who pulled the trigger on the man who 'had a dream' but a mega-plot, orchestrated by nameless, invisible forces, generated in the dark corridors of power, and executed with demonic stealth. We can't quite bear our heroes to fall victims to commonplace, random nastiness.

But figures like Martin Luther King don't float above the events of their times, with their best speech polished in their pocket, waiting for the last scene of the last act, which leads to death and apotheosis. Their lives are not operas, but daily struggles with trivia and paperwork; shaking hands, placating egos, answering thousands of letters and phone calls, weighing risks, developing strategies, and trying not to lose their souls in the tide of admiration they inspire. They *become* great through the normal tedious routes of politics and persuasion, and what finishes them is often as unplanned as an untied shoe-lace. What it took to kill King was a grudge, a gun and an opportunity.

We should not indulge too easily in conspiracy theories because they are bad for us. This week Christians are preoccupied with another great death, the death of Jesus Christ. It was an obscure event in its time – hardly noticed by contemporary historians. In trying to understand why Jesus was killed, his followers worked up a massive conspiracy theory against the Jewish race; a theory which has cast a long shadow over our history. Even today we're only just beginning to get free of it. I think the death of Jesus was probably more a cock-up than a plot, a combination of provocation and fear; an overcrowded city, a sadistic Roman governor, a cautious hgh priest who made a thoroughly sensible, but utterly catastrophic decision. Our fates rest on such small things; which means we are always engaged by them and always responsible. It is out of the random and the trivial that the judgement of God comes to meet us; the straight script written in lines as crooked as the human heart.

GOOD FRIDAY IN NORTHERN IRELAND

13 April 1998

In the midst of all the excitement about Northern Ireland I've found it quite sobering to listen to reactions from people who live there. I remember the ecstatic relief which greeted the initial IRA ceasefire. But this time there's a stunned caution about. People sound only just hopeful, as though they can't quite believe there's been a breakthrough. We've been disappointed so many times that we don't know how to get our minds round the possibility of success. The habit of unbelief dies hard.

I was thinking about this yesterday, when as a deacon in the first year since my ordination I sang in church the 'Easter Proclamation' – an elaborate unaccompanied chant in praise of the resurrection. It's got lots of difficult transitions and twirly bits in the music, and I have to confess that when I was first asked to do it my heart quailed.

Just over a week ago I started to practise. I got the plainsong written out in ordinary notes and found a key that I could manage the high bits and the low bits in. For days I stumbled over it, losing the pitch or finding I couldn't fit the words together right. I tried dinning it into my head by going over the same phrase again and again. I sang it as I did the ironing, the music propped up before me. I listened to a tape while I was in my car. Very gradually the words and musical patterns began to get hold of me. They even penetrated my sleep. By now the sheet music was covered with coffee stains and pencil markings, and even the remnants of sun-dried tomatoes; a witness to the fact that it had accompanied me everywhere. And then suddenly on Saturday I sang it all the way through and found that the chant was there; beginning to take on its own life, to sing itself through me. 'Rejoice heavenly powers, sing choirs of angels . . .' I'd seen the 'Easter Proclamation' as a technical challenge; and yet suddenly here it was, speaking to me of hope and forgiveness, and of the joy that death has been overcome. Even our fundamental sin is seen as a blessing; because through it has come our great redeemer.

In Northern Ireland, these last weeks and months have been hard work. The long process has dinned in the words and the music: the subtle notes of compromise, the undernotes of trust, the high notes of hope. But now the peace must sing itself. The vision must take fire. The 'Easter Proclamation' ends with words which apply to all our strivings for peace, in Northern Ireland and everywhere: 'May the morning star which never sets find this flame still burning: Christ that morning star who came back from the dead and sheds his peaceful light on humankind.'

CREATOR AND PAEDOPHILE

20 April 1998

Sex, art and religion are a pretty potent mix. Eric Gill was a letter cutter and a stonemason. Eighty-five years ago he got a commission from Westminster Cathedral to make fourteen carved panels showing the journey of Jesus to the cross. These stations of the cross are a focus for prayer: you wander from one to the other, following the Passion story. Gill was a devout Catholic but he was also a paedophile who had incest with his sisters and his daughters. For those who carry memories of abuse, his work has become a visual blasphemy. They claim that the man cannot be separated from his art, and that the panels should be removed. Others say that the art is independent of the artist, and that they should remain. It would be easier to resolve this dilemma if Gill had accepted a moral gap between his art and his life. After all, plenty of notorious sinners have produced magnificent art for the Church. But Gill believed in the integrity of what he did. He was something of a theologian. He loved the verse of John's Gospel which says that 'The Word became flesh and dwelt among us.' The flesh, to him, was therefore holy, and human love in all its varieties was an echo of divine love.

I can see why some might want to remove the panels, to eradicate the mingling of the Passion of Christ with human passions we now condemn. But I couldn't go that far. They are, in their own way, beautiful, striking works. People still pray with them. The problem for us is how to live with the fact that they were carved by hands which also sinned so grievously against innocent flesh.

I don't find this easy. I want to believe that true religion is good for us. Yet every day brings stories of violence and abuse in church vestries and Christian schools. I have found myself wondering whether there isn't something inherently sadistic in a religion which has the cross at its centre and speaks of God dying in agony to win our human love. Is it surprising that some kinky souls are led astray?

When I think of Eric Gill's work I see something of the huge riskiness of Christian faith. Christianity is an emotional religion. It is about reason *and* passion, the redemption of the flesh as well as the salvation of the soul. Perhaps it is when it is most inspired that it also has most potential to wound. We live on a knife edge, for which the only remedy is a daily awareness of our own capacity for harm. The cross is a terrible symbol; but only because it is so terrible can it speak to the sinner and the sinned against both of God's judgement on the crimes of the flesh and of his inexhaustible mercy.

NO FINAL SOLUTIONS

27 April 1998

'Shalom Yisrael' (Peace be on Israel) on the fiftieth anniversary of the Israeli state. The conflicts of our world all seem to be to do with land, who owns it, who controls it, who is dispossessed in order to secure it. It would be nice to think that this is a modern problem, but we are restless animals on this planet of ours, and people have always moved about in search of a better life. What we call civilization is the fruit of endless struggles for territory.

I am not convinced that people are capable of making lasting peace out of idealism. We're rather good at dreams, of course, and peace on earth is a wonderful aspiration, but experience suggests peace is only secure when it comes from self-interest.

I'm always struck by the way English history used to be taught as a succession of catastrophes followed by peaceful settlements. First the ancient Britons, then the Romans, then the Saxons, then the Vikings, then the Normans: each wave of invaders sailing grimly across the Channel or over the North Sea with fire and the sword. Every invasion wreaked havoc, people lost their homes and lives. But nothing is ever neat or tidy and there are no total conquests, no final solutions. Conquerors and vanquished damaged each other terribly, but in the end they became one. Sexual attraction helps of course; people will go on falling in love with their enemies. We also have a crafty way of doing deals with our opponents to enhance our position within our own group. And the result of all this human messiness is that we still share Celtic memories and psychology, Viking names and red hair, Saxon and Latin and Norman French all over our language. We are a series of peoples that have been bashed about by each other and somehow come out of it with more than we would have had if we had stayed an isolated people. And though I hope that in these islands the age of violence is past, I also hope that we will go on changing.

Yet much in our modern ideologies expects peace to be the fruit of purity. Ethnicity has come to carry a kind of sacred charge, as though it's become wrong to ever intermarry or convert to another faith, because such decisions mess about with our desire to be clear about the politics of living space. But from such crossings-over have come the greatest blessings. Ruth the Moabite, following her mother-in-law Naomi into the land of Israel took to herself Israel's people and their god and she became the ancestor of Israel's greatest king. Is there something here of the providence of God who scatters our idealism to the winds and forces us to deal with each other as the cunning, creative, desiring creatures that we actually are?

———————

MEETING OF FAITHS

10 August 1998

Islam is a growing force in the world and it's one we need to understand. The bombings in Nairobi and Dar-es-Salaam have tweaked our fear of terrorism inspired by militant faith. But that's not the whole story. At the Lambeth Conference, which ended yesterday, I heard Anglican bishops talk about living close to Islam in Africa, Asia, the Middle East and here in Britain. Some had tales of persecution. Others, of ancient friendship between the faiths. Some claimed to be as sure of the truth of the Bible as Muslims are about the Koran. In and through the debate was the unspoken question: is Islam of God? And if it is, where do Christians stand?

My first real encounter with Islam was over twenty years ago. I had visited Mombasa on the east coast of Kenya, and had been introduced to a young Muslim scholar. He made me a gift of the Koran, with Arabic on one side of the page and Swahili on the other – a beautifully bound green volume with gold lettering. He then asked me whether I understood that Islam was the supreme religion, the last revelation. He asked if I was truly happy in myself and whether I had ever considered converting from Christianity to the true faith. I remember feeling vaguely affronted; not because he was in any way aggressive, but because I recognized that the things he was saying about Islam I believed to be true of Christianity. In the event, natural and English reticence held me back from fighting my corner, but his conviction forced me to face the fact that I *did* simply assume that my own religion was the top religion and that others would be better off converting to it, rather than me to theirs.

I thought the two faiths could only ever be rivals; fighting each other for the same space in the human soul. Yet as I went on thinking about the conversation, the irony of it got through to me. I, the convinced Christian, had been the object of another person's missionary endeavour! Since then I have been a little less certain that there is only one way to God. I have come to find in Islam a marvellous spaciousness and order, a sense of God's calm beauty and everlasting compassion. But it's not only the things which are *like* Christianity which I value – it's the difference. In Islam, God is both remote and close, but he is always other; there's no incarnation. I can't reconcile the two faiths in my head, but somehow I think that the difference is a holy space where we learn to listen before talking. As some of the Anglican bishops showed me, unpressured encounter is the only alternative to the assumed superiority which begins in persuasion and can sometimes end in a terrorist bomb.

MONEY AND THE QUEEN

19 October 1998

When Members of Parliament pray for the Queen today they'll use a new prayer which leaves out the traditional petition for her wealth. Instead they'll ask for her well-being; which I suppose means health, happiness and the modest prosperity which most of us aspire to. It sounds like a trivial change; the Queen will still be prayed for as 'our gracious sovereign lady'; she is still to be given strength to 'vanquish her enemies' and to 'attain everlasting joy and felicity' after the struggles of this earthly life. But earthly wealth is out.

Why, I wonder? Is it because she's wealthy enough, and to ask the Almighty day after day to add financial security to all other gifts and graces seems superfluous? Is it that it is simply preposterous (hear the tone of moral indignation) to ask God for royal wealth while some of her subjects are begging in the street?

Or is it more complicated than that, a kind of inadmissible

envy? Three hundred years ago when Parliamentary prayers were instituted it was obvious that a functioning monarchy would be a healthy and wealthy one. The monarch's wealth and health would represent God's blessing on the whole nation; we would all have a symbolic share in it. It would stand for the generosity of God in our national life. The fact that a lot of people were poor and hungry didn't make the monarch's wealth inappropriate; it made it even more necessary. A poor monarch, scrabbling for funds, would have been shameful. But now we find it hard to understand how wealth can be representative. We're simply not interested in reflected glory; we take it personally. What she has, we don't. Her wealth cuts us out, like disinherited children. We want the Queen to worry about her tax return as we have to; to see her savings and shares go up and down in value, to have to balance the books.

And if there's anything left over, we don't see why we should not have some of the royal bounty, or if that thought makes our envy transparent, we say we think it ought to go to our under-funded hospitals and schools.

The Bible is very clear about the dangers of wealth for our spiritual life; the love of money is the root of all evil. But we hear less these days of the other biblical message; that prosperity can be received as a blessing of God for which we should all be thankful. Wealth has become simply godless; you can be rich or holy, but not both. Money is a very, very private matter – more private than sex or prayer; and the fact that we can no longer pray for the Queen's wealth suggests that it is at least possible that one of the evils gripping us today is an excessive love of the stuff.

TOO OLD TO
SUFFER PUNISHMENT?

25 October 1998

General Pinochet lies in his bed waiting to know his fate. Over his prone figure the arguments rage about his release or extradition. Should old tyrants be made to pay for their crimes? If not, where is justice for their victims? If so, what possible punishment can provide that justice, given that this old tyrant is now sick and powerless? Does God come down on the side of justice at all costs or does God favour a pragmatic forgiveness?

What everyone wants is some sort of exorcism, a re-ordering of the past. The ghosts of dread are out on the streets in Chile and Spain, and over the General's bed hovers the question: how do we return to some sort of order? Surely God remembers the past, and requires us to do so too, so that we can mend our ways.

The Pinochet regime was not an aberration. He came to power with rough but solid ideals, and aims which others shared. A strict Catholic, he tried to impose order on the economic nightmare Chile had become. He reckoned that the loss of human rights was a legitimate price to pay. So the guns and the goosestep, the dark glasses and brassy uniforms, the booming economy – and the secret atrocities. It's clear that Pinochet has not the imagination to recant. He still believes that he did his best to do his duty to God and his nation. When he realized he'd failed, he managed a dignified departure, leaving his country to create a new democratic order.

The Spanish judge who now accuses him is also concerned for order; he wants Pinochet tried in the name of the Spanish victims who died or disappeared in those grim years. British subjects also suffered under Pinochet, and live with the damage to their minds and bodies. It would all be so much easier if the former dictator was fit and well and could suffer a bit. But now he is helpless, what would restore order, for his victims and for Chile's future, is not so clear.

Time has moved on and there is a real risk that violence could be struck from these dying embers of the old man's life. So the moral question now is not, how can the wrongs of the past be righted – because in some sense they simply cannot be. But there's a more modest question: how to restore order so that the brutal past does not create a brutal future. I'm drawn back to the Bible, to its sense of the fragility of human order and the need – before either strict justice or pragmatism – to remember God. Vengeance is mine, I will repay, says the Lord. General Pinochet still has to meet his God, as do we. Today and every day we are accountable for our deeds.

THE DARK SIDE

2 November 1998

Ted Hughes died last week, the best poet for years to be Poet Laureate. On my twenty-first birthday I was given a volume of his work: not a pretty, gift book, but *The Life and Songs of Crow*. Poems about the black, scavenger bird that circles the country-side with its maniac caw. When I opened the book I was startled by its savagery. Crow is born of scream and blood and blackness; he lives on grubs, crusts, anything. He is part of a horrifying creation, he kills and is unkillable. He argues with a sad God and wins. He has no hope or pity, only a jaunty, obscene humour, and he survives against the odds. On All Souls' Day when we remember the inevitability of death – our own death – I find I want to make space for Ted Hughes and his poetry.

He was a big man, a Yorkshireman, who loved the wildness of nature: the wind and rain, the cries of life feeding off life. He saw violence as the raw energy of a hostile universe. He managed to put in fierce words what so many people of this century feel about life – that it's a pretty bloody business. God is apparently impotent; love, no more than a blind rush of bodies, and death rules everything. What is strange is how calm you feel after reading all this. You know that at the very least he has told you his truth. Tragedy expressed without pity or sentimentality has a healing quality. Like the water he describes which longs to live, but can only weep: 'It finally lay at the bottom of all things, utterly worn out, utterly clear.'

Hughes was married to Sylvia Plath, a gifted poet in love with death, who killed herself as she always seems to have known she would. Only this year, after years of silence, Hughes published his Birthday Letters, a memorial which reveals his love for her. This poet of the wilderness was also surprisingly tender-hearted, vulnerable, much more human than his work might suggest. As we all are. Beneath the bravado, the caw of the hungry black crow, who devours all and survives all, lies human nature, with its wonder and heartbreak. He said little of that, perhaps, but he lived it.

Today I will go to the altar in our small community chapel and read the names of the dead, commending them to God's mercy. Somehow I do believe in a God who embraces the life of Crow and redeems it; who honours the poet's witness to the darkness of things, and yet entices us to dream: of the forgiveness of all sins and the life everlasting.

WARIS DIRIE AND
MONICA LEWINSKY

8 March 1999

In the secular calendar it's International Women's Day. I'm not sure whether to keep it as a feast or a fast. To celebrate the advancement of women or to meditate on the amount of female suffering that still goes on all over the world.

Today two particular woman are making me ask how far we are able to see female persons in their biblical dignity as the image of the true God. I think first of Waris Dirie, a Somali from a nomadic tribe. At the age of twelve she fled an arranged marriage to a sixty-year-old stranger who had five camels to give for her. A good price, apparently. By astonishing luck she got herself to London and was discovered by a fashion photographer. That was the beginning of a stunning career as an international model. Yet she was mutilated at the age of five and carries the scars of that for ever. At the time, she was told that the pain would cleanse her and make her fit for marriage. Now she campaigns for the United Nations for an end to female circumcision. She was shown this weekend cradling her baby son, an icon of black and female dignity and beauty. She believes God helped her survive. And it occurred to me that it might be very much part of God's work to redeem women and men from sexual enslavement. Which isn't just an issue for the developing world.

There's the other female icon of the week: Monica. She's signing copies of her book in Harrods today, and I wonder how many who go will take a strange and thrilling pleasure in seeing the woman . . . who . . . and yet how pert and, in her brittle way, dignified she is too. She seems content with her lot. Pleased with her story. After all, she has gained what many women desire because they don't really have it: attention.

I think I'm arguing myself into keeping this day as a fast and not a feast. For it seems to me that we cannot condemn the physical mutilation of women in the developing world if we don't also see our part in the mental mutilation that brings us Monica: there's a woman with all the benefits of Western technology, education and culture. Yet so naïve and unprotected that she thinks she can find love by flashing her knickers at a vain sex-hog of a President. It's not much better than being exchanged for five camels.

And yet we are all players in her story: President, prosecutor, ghost-writer, press, preacher. We are exposed by what we most condemn and must repent before we see salvation. Earnest prayer I think, and lentils for supper.

FALKLANDS QUESTIONS

15 March 1999

Prince Charles's visit to the Falklands brought back memories of the war of 1982. Grey, swollen seas and flaring Exocets. Baffled-looking sheep peering at close-cropped helmets. And the funeral of Colonel H. Jones who died a hero's death at Goose Green. The Falklands War is now a legend, a defensive war, justly won. On its strength the islanders remain defiantly opposed to any compromise over British sovereignty. In fact they're much more opposed now than they were before General Galtieri's invasion.

It could all so easily have been otherwise. If it hadn't been for that extraordinary Argentinian miscalculation, history might have taken a very different turn. The islanders' claim has never been beyond dispute. The British gained these grey lumps of rock from eighteenth-century piracy. The first inhabitants, apart from wailing birds, were remnants of a naval garrison who thought the place so awful no one would mind them staying, until a Spanish force arrived and tried to dislodge them. The moral base of our sovereignty is nothing more elevated than the fact that 'we were here first'. At the end of the 1970s the Foreign Office was gently moving things along to a peaceful compromise. It was reckoned that the islanders, already dependent on Buenos Aires for serious schools, hospitals and anything but basic shopping, would have gradually accepted an erosion of independence as a commonsense exchange for convenience. But the war changed all that.

One of the principles of fighting a just war is that it should be winnable. This is not just a pragmatic principle, it is a moral one as well. To fight a just war you have to believe in your cause and you have to be prepared to sacrifice lives. But just as important, you have to be pretty sure you can win. 'What king,' asked Jesus, 'going to encounter another king in war, will not sit down first and take counsel whether he is able with ten thousand to meet him who comes to him with twenty thousand? And if not, while the other is yet a great way off, he sends an embassy and asks for peace.'

The Falklands War was quickly over. For all the heroism it was arguably a war that should never have been. It has left Britain with its sovereignty set in stone, but on as morally flaky a base as it ever was. Yesterday's celebrations made me uneasy, because they reminded me of the stupidity of fighting wars for show. I wonder how many of today's conflicts are ideological theatre, costly media exercises which have no conclusion because they cannot be won by either side. To count the cost before setting out to fight is not only common sense; it's a moral brake on the death and heartache of wars drummed up by nothing more than vanity.

MANDELA IN
THE VALE OF MISERY

16 June 1999

As Thabo Mbeki is sworn in as South Africa's President today, Nelson Mandela stands down. Mandela is a world hero of course; but he's also been called a secular saint. People see qualities in him which go beyond political vision and charismatic leadership. They see integrity: the fruits of hard, inner, self-discipline. It all started in those long, apparently wasted years on Robben Island. Before his imprisonment he was an angry man. Rightly, given the injustices he was up against. But in isolation he became convinced that anger was a luxury that he could no longer afford. He set himself to conquer his temper. That was only the beginning. The prison system was designed to tear away at self-confidence and self-respect. The point was to get him to internalize his own sentence; to become as bitter and violent as the judgement on him. But he managed to see through that strategy and turn it on its head. So instead of fantasizing about the revenge he would have on his thuggish jailors, he made the impossible leap of trying to see them as civilized human beings. Over the years his efforts paid off. Slowly and painfully, day by day, he converted his enemies. He made them into something like reasonable people.

Of course he had to mean it. It couldn't just be rhetoric or spin. When you're sent off to hammer stones all day in the blazing heat; when your eyes ache from the glare of the sun, and you know you're going slowly blind; when you're fed on disgusting slops and yelled at, mere spin gets a bit thin. First he had to pretend not to hate the brutes who tormented him; then by acting as though he didn't hate them, he began to pretend to like them. For pretend, read practise.

His secret was humility, which is not grovelling, but clear-sightedness. Evil can be undone only by its opposite, and in

34

normal life we have no time for that, so we settle for checking and containing it as best we can. But the isolation of Robben Island gave Mandela all the time in the world to experiment with evil's undoing. His cell was a laboratory of the spirit, as truly as any monk's cell with its crucifix on the wall. A tribute to Mandela would be to use our adversities more creatively than we want to, to convert any great or petty injustices done against us into unexpected virtue. There are those, according to the Psalms, whose strength in God enables them to do that: 'Blessed is the man whose strength is in thee: in whose heart are thy ways, who going through the vale of misery use it for a well: and the pools are filled with water.'

A FEW MISSING MIRACLES

26 July 1999

It's less than two years since her death, but Mother Teresa is already on her way to beatification, the first major step to sainthood. Today, after a ceremony in Calcutta, a committee will be set up to investigate her life, and if all goes well, she will become the Blessed Mother Teresa.

I know I should feel pleased about it, and in a way I do. This wicked world can always do with more saints. Ever since Malcolm Muggeridge stumbled into her home for the dying with a wobbly camera and a tired old sinner's desire for evidence of God, she has been an icon of holiness. She's also been attacked, for naïveté, for old-fashioned practices, for getting money from unsavoury sources. All this needs to be looked at. The complication for the investigators is that Mother Teresa is not an obscure figure. She's already known to billions. She's a media star. And the Church seems to be happy with that, rushing through this beatification as though it were a scoop. The usual five years which ought to lapse after a holy person's death have, in her case, been cut. The usual requirement for miracles has been waived. It all sounds as if there is a determination that Mother Teresa should have her halo by the millennium.

And that's where I have a problem. What is impressive about Catholicism is the way it blends passionate devotion with rigorous theology. You can have all sorts of mystical experiences, you can serve the needs of the world until your hands are calloused and your feet swollen up, but in the end there has to be a cool weighing of evidence that goes beyond any needs we might have. When there are strong claims being made, the Church's task is to urge caution.

In the days after her death, Princess Diana was treated as a saint, with spontaneous prayer in the streets and wayside shrines and candles and flowers; but after a year we found the shrines quietly dismantled. She settled into our memories as the hysteria faded. Mother Teresa is a much more serious candidate for sainthood, but why should she be exempt from the judgement of time?

I fear for a Church that has lost confidence in its own slow wisdom, a Church that apes the media-driven world in making instant judgements on complicated lives, producing new saints as though to prove its own powers. Whatever happened to eternity? And the God for whom a thousand years are but a day?

A decent lapse of time can do no harm. We need saints, but we need them to be deep and real. A five- or ten-year gap might even leave time for a few missing miracles.

SHRINKS ON HOLIDAY

2 August 1999

All over middle-class London, from Hampstead to Notting Hill, Clapham Common to Wimbledon, in media land and business land, among teachers and carers and creatives, clergy and journalists and academics – this is Black Monday. It's the first working day in August, and August is that cruellest of months when the shrinks go on holiday. No more analysis, counselling, therapy for four weeks and a bit. Today clients are asking: how can someone who I pay to care for me actually leave me for something so trivial as a holiday? Aren't my problems enough to satisfy? Or, what have I done to my shrink to make them need to go away? The guilty, the greedy, the neurotic, the needy and the plain sad – all of us who have ever needed to be listened to professionally – are left with these questions. Alas, what August points to is the exhaustion factor in human caring. Even the best of shrinks cannot be everything. Unconditional positive regard may be the alchemy of healing, but you can't have it available twelve months of the year. The well has dried up and needs to be replenished.

I expect Freud and Jung started it with their summer retreats. They always look so leisured in photographs beside lakes and mountains and well-kept gardens. They took their clients with them, which must have made for a jolly holiday. Part of the mystique of therapy is what is concealed from the client, and there's plenty of time in August to fantasize about your shrink, wondering whether they're sobbing in a darkened room or living it up in night clubs; flat out on the beach or hiking through the Himalayas. Do they tell other people what they do, when they meet on a cruise or in the jacuzzi? Do they ever think of you? It's a nice thought for an abandoned client to picture his shrink chewing fingernails by a swimming pool, longing to be back. Or is it a secret relief that the shrink's gone away? Time to play, to forget to remember your dreams, to forget to worry about death?

Yesterday there was a baptism in my church in the scorching heat. The water flowing into the font reminded me that our great faiths come from the desert, where all that stands between life and death is water. No wonder water becomes a symbol of life itself, and then of God's life. Carl Gustav Jung was a great healer, but he believed that the neurosis we suffer from comes essentially from our spiritual shallowness, our lack of contact with God.

Perhaps August is a retreat for those who care, and those who are cared for, to learn not to care for a bit, to let ourselves just be in that divine ocean which permeates all things and creates and renews all things. The water that springs to eternal life never runs dry.

LENIN'S TOMB

9 August 1999

President Yeltsin wants to bury Vladimir Ilich Lenin. Since 1924 the embalmed body of the founder of the Soviet Union has lain in Moscow in a granite mausoleum in its old-fashioned suit and tie and cufflinks. There's something undeniably arresting about Lenin's mortal remains. The domed head, moustache and shining fingernails, the skin kept moist and soft.

If the President gets his way, the body will be quietly removed, flown to St Petersburg and buried beside the grave of Lenin's mother. Lenin the great and terrible will come home. Dust to dust, ashes to ashes. There'll be protests of course, for burying Lenin will be seen as a kind of desecration, a symbolic attempt to bury Communism. It will be seen as drawing a line under one of the most daring of social experiments to be tried, and to fail, in the course of human history.

Whatever the political arguments for and against letting Lenin go to his rest, there are compelling spiritual reasons. He has been close to a god in the memory and imagination of millions, the embodiment of the strong and ruthless leader that Russia has always yearned for. His vision, though ruthlessly implemented, was humane; he really wanted a society of justice and equality. A disciplined state and a nation of disciplined selves. He was something of an ascetic in his personal habits, driven by the lifelong task of making his vision real. But like all human gods, Lenin's divinity was his downfall, and his triumph in the October Revolution ushered in not peace, but terror. While his body still reigns from his granite tomb it is difficult to imagine a new future or any kind of future for this tragic and corrupted nation.

Lenin needs his funeral, and so do his people. In fact we all need funerals and partings to mark the fact of death. As the earth is piled in over the coffin or the curtains close around there is an almost heart-stopping moment of grief, and sometimes panic and terror, especially for those who feel most lost and betrayed, whose faith in life has been smashed. But without a ritual departure the death is not complete and the bereaved can't free themselves from the influence of the dead.

Perhaps it is hard for the godless to believe this, and the Communist Party of Russia will hate it. Preserving the body of a great figurehead is an attempt to cheat death, to tie up the future so nothing can change. Yet the empire has crumbled and now the all-too-human emperor must face the judgement and the mercy of history. We will all see more clearly how Lenin was great when he has completed the life-cycle as the rest of us have to, from cradle to grave. Perhaps out of his postponed death, three-quarters of a century on, could come the resurrection of a great people.

SUMMER OF LOVE

16 August 1999

Remember the summer of love thirty years ago? The drifting Indian ragas and flowers in your hair? Dropping out and tuning in? Well, no, I missed it. In 1969 I was nineteen and just about to go up to Cambridge. As I prepared earnestly for student life in my black polo neck jumper and Mary Whitehouse glasses, I thought my spaced-out elders rather silly. I knew all there was to know about what really mattered: God, morality and human progress. These were much more important than a load of unwashed hippies.

Sensible people like me lived in the head with an eye to the future. We dreamed of having stable, everlasting marriages and secure, happy children. We hoped to build a society that was just and rational. I could tell you then what constituted Christian behaviour. The Ten Commandments were a blueprint for daily living and before going to church it was a duty to search one's conscience, not only to check if you'd murdered anyone or committed adultery, but also to confess any angry or lustful thought that might have flickered across the screen of the mind. It was noble and high-minded, and it's half of who I am.

But then I tried living it out. And I found that the summer of love had not been something other people did. It had curled its way into my life like incense, a whiff of mystery and excitement, that said living from the mind is only half a life. God is in the heart, not only in the head, in our intuition not our reason, in being who we are, not doing what we've been told is right. I found that living so earnestly had become not only boring but dangerous. It made me pretend to attitudes I found I couldn't hold, to commitments I couldn't fulfil. On a wider scale I began to see the horror that lay behind societies claimed to be built on pure reason. The oppression, the manipulation, the corruption. The lack of mercy for human fallibility and playfulness.

Gradually I became attuned to what sounded at first like worryingly permissive voices from the Christian tradition. Julian of Norwich saying that God looks on us with pity, not with blame. Augustine with his astonishing command: love God, then do what you like. So they became part of me too.

There is now for me an inner conversation between the child of the 1950s and the 1960s: the rationalist and the romantic. As I look back over these thirty years I would not have had it otherwise. There's fracture and human damage everywhere: too much head stuff, too much pure sensation. But the art of salvation is to bring the two together, to find the image of God again in society and our deepest selves; but this time, restored and renewed.

NAKED CIVIL SERVANT

24 November 1999

Quentin Crisp died on Sunday – the 'stately homo of England' as he rather grandly styled himself. From the obituaries his picture surveys us with weary amusement. The made-up face framed by the lilac hair and battered trilby, dainty shirt and chiffon scarf. His arched eyebrows seem to be asking us if we are still shocked by his antics. He was ninety and for years had dreamed of death. He said he wanted the fame of being murdered, though he wasn't. Instead he'll be missed.

Inside Quentin Crisp was a serious question: *Who would you be if there was no praise or blame?* He tried to live the answer to his question: to imagine, in an age which hated effeminacy, that there was no finger-pointing mockery, at a time before gay rights were invented, that he was nobody's victim. He defined his task in life as being simply, resolutely, defiantly himself. For this he was ridiculed and beaten up, ejected from homes and denied jobs. He learnt to bear injustice and to go on and on flaunting his peculiarities until *we* learnt to be more tolerant. Over the years people began to see in him, not bravado but real bravery, something almost akin to saintliness.

The question he asked is important, perhaps the most important question there is. *Who would you be if there was no praise or blame?* All the spiritual traditions tell us to know ourselves and yet our self-knowledge is often constructed from other people's opinions. We want to be praised and fear to be censured, and while we are pulled between the two, our sense of self fluctuates between self-approval and self-hatred. Even God becomes part of the cycle of praise and blame; looking after us when we're good, bashing us when we're bad.

There's a popular spiritual experiment in which you try to write two obituaries of yourself. One you write as if you were your greatest enemy; the other as a sympathetic friend. As you compare and contrast the two accounts you begin to realize that they are written not only about the same person but by the same person. You are these two selves. You are your own judge and your own advocate. With that insight comes freedom. I think Quentin Crisp went through a version of that process when he decided to live flamboyantly, as a figure of disgrace.

It's a paradox that what he shows me is something about grace. Grace is not a reward for goodness nor a rescue from badness. It is simply that dangerous freedom to be who you are. In religious language, a justified sinner. Or perhaps even that most inconceivable of heroes – a naked civil servant.

DOING THE UNTHINKABLE

15 December 1999

In a few hours from now the Israeli Prime Minister will start the next round of talks with Syria. Ehud Barak wants to return the Golan Heights which Israel seized in the six-day war and later annexed. Yesterday seven thousand Israelis were out on the streets with placards saying 'Stop Giving Away Our Country to Terrorists'.

Yet no one can claim that the Golan was ever really part of Israel. In the Hebrew Bible, Syria is a hostile, threatening power. I remember how this came home to me once when I was standing on the south side of the Sea of Galilee under the lowering cliffs of the Golan. You could imagine farmers and fishermen of biblical times looking with fear on those hills. Over them could come the Syrian forces with bows and arrows and horsemen. And they did come, according to the second book of Kings – fierce raiding parties, year after year in the springtime.

Even in New Testament times, Syria remains other, impenetrably foreign. The Gospels describe Jesus crossing the Sea of Galilee into the weird land of the Gerasenes where there were unclean tombs and chained-up madmen who thought they were armies, and where, as any first-century Jewish peasant knew all too well, the Roman legions were stationed, ready to march across into Galilee and beyond at any hint of trouble. Jesus goes as an exorcist. He cures a possessed man by driving his demons into a herd of pigs who topple themselves over the cliffs and into the sea. This causes so much panic that the locals beg him to go away.

A few years ago I visited an orthodox kibbutz in Galilee. I learnt how in its early days the settlers had been relentlessly fired on by Syrian guns hidden in the hills. After the six-day war they had rejoiced in Israel's annexation of the Golan. Security at last, they thought. But over the years they had gone through a slow change of heart. They desperately wanted security, of course, but not at such a high moral cost. They had come to see that there was a relationship between occupying the Golan and failing to find peace with their immediate Arab neighbours. Those settlers were prepared to think the unthinkable, to give up the Golan.

It will be a profoundly hard decision for Israel to carry through. If it happens, many will lose their homes. There will be bitterness and anxiety, and a sense of betrayal, and other potential losses too, not least a wonderful red Shiraz from the Golan vineyards. Yet sometimes it is only by facing an enemy without that we are able to come to terms with the enemy we most fear, the enemy within. If Israel can face those dark hills of otherness, perhaps there is a chance for peace inside her ancient borders.

MYRA HINDLEY

1 March 2000

Will we ever get over the 'moors murders'? Ian Brady is pleading for the right to die. On TV tonight we'll debate whether Myra Hindley could ever be released. The papers churn out the old defiant mugshots of the two; the relatives of the victims make their usual protest, and we all rake over the embers for little sparks of new detail, as fascinated as we are appalled.

There's no way out, it seems. Victims, murderers, relatives of victims, media and press, and all of us are obsessed by these murders, and we see no resolution, no ending. Myra Hindley has a brain disease and Ian Brady is trying to starve to death. And that's caused a new panic, with the possible deaths of the perpetrators being trumpeted as the devil's cleverest ploy. How dare they simply die, and cheat us once again!

And yet all life is living and dying. Nothing lasts for ever. The endless extension of the present moment is not heaven but hell, that eternal hell Jesus warned of – where we are all fixed for ever in our sins because we refuse to let go, to be changed.

I find myself trying to imagine what the 'moors murders' look like from the perspective of eternity. We used to believe in God, not just in private, but in public, and that made a difference. It didn't take the sting from tragedy, but it did help us to accept that life goes on. Our problem is that when we think of the child victims it is as though the needle of time has stuck, and we hear them still crying for mercy after thirty years. If only we believed, we would be able to set alongside that past horror a sure and certain hope that they are now free from pain and healed and at peace. There is transformation beyond this life.

If we believed in God we might have been able to accept the earthly punishment of Hindley and Brady without expecting it to be the last word. If the death sentence had been in force, the judge would have asked God's mercy on their souls, but to show concern to the two in life is howled down as wimpishness. If we believed, we might have been able to accept that it is human faces like ours which wear the incomprehensible masks of the devil. Don't the papers go on printing their pictures, and don't we go on looking, precisely because we need to learn this? So God have mercy on our souls too. And even, I think, for the poor relatives there might have been some way, not of forgetting, or even forgiving, but of simply leaving the final word to God, a safer refuge than the frantic, overloaded hells of our own memories. Memory is a tribute to the dead, but it can also be a prison – and it is from this prison that all of us, and not only Ian Brady, need release.

MUGABE AND MARXISM

14 April 2000

Twenty years ago Robert Gabriel Mugabe won a landslide election victory to become Prime Minister of the new republic of Zimbabwe. I remember the warm words with which the Thatcher government greeted his triumph, the ecstasy of the political left, and also how delighted my more zealous Christian friends were, rejoicing in the fact that the handsome, scholarly Mugabe was a practising Catholic. It was the year of the murder of Archbishop Oscar Romero in El Salvador, and liberation theology was much in vogue. Mugabe seemed purer on all fronts than his political opponents. He had both a lively faith and an agenda for justice. When he said, as he did, that when he came to power 'none of the white exploiters would be allowed to keep an acre of land', it seemed unexceptional, obvious. To take up arms on behalf of the poor, to liberate the oppressed from wealthy élites was a clear corollary of belief in the gospel.

Yet what is happening today doesn't have that moral clarity. The country is split – as yesterday's judicial judgement reveals. The ragged army of the landless with their pangas and brooms are comic and frightening by turns. They seem less an army of the righteous poor than a pathetic crew, dancing to empty promises. The white farmers with blood on their faces seem dignified and resigned, trying to stay within the law, touched by the loyalties the crisis has evoked.

I wonder if we'll look back on these months and see them as the end of the long romance between Christianity and Marxism? I was never pure enough twenty years ago to be a Marxist, though I hoped to be counted as a Christian. But I could see the attraction of it all at the time; the thrill of reading the gospel, of feeding the hungry and raising the poor and thinking you could actually make it happen. Prayer, study, right thought, correct praxis and the kingdom of God will draw near. It's wonderful. But there was always a dark side.

Christianity and Marxism are both totalitarian. Christianity in its claim for God, Marxism in its claim on people. Recently Christians have been more cautious about claiming to be right about everything. There have even been apologies for past wrongs. But something of that gleam, that fascination with absolute power, returns when Christians find themselves in sympathy with a coercive ideology. Zimbabwe is reaping the bitter fruit of that love affair. And those of us who were seduced by its magic twenty years ago need to learn from what is happening there. There is Gospel wisdom in keeping a critical gap between faith and politics. It's where humour comes in, and kindness, and space to be disillusioned and recover. It is not too late to compromise. It is never too late to repent.

CHRIST AND JUDAS

21 April 2000 (Good Friday)

On Tuesday I went to the National Gallery to see the much-hyped exhibition 'Seeing Salvation'. It was packed with visitors, damp from the afternoon rain, shuffling past images of the sad, scourged, suffering Christ. Hot and airless, we trudged past the cruel nails and crown of thorns all graphically displayed. I was just about to flake out when I entered a room where an even denser crowd had gathered. Curious, I edged my way in. They were gazing at four small ivory carvings from the early fifth century. I looked. What I saw was four more scenes from the Passion of Christ. But these were different. One of them was a very early, perhaps the earliest, depiction of the crucifixion. The cross fills the right hand of the panel. Christ is squat and muscular, nailed bolt upright, staring without expression, like a soldier on guard, stoic and solid, showing no pain.

On the left of the panel is a tree in full leaf. A bird has built a nest and is feeding her young in a branch. The branch is weighed over to the right, and from it, at the end of a taut rope, is a hanged man. The head is yanked up by the rope, the hands and feet dangle listlessly. At the foot of the tree, big round coins are spilling out of the bag. This is Judas, the betrayer.

I find it astonishing that over fifteen hundred years ago an anonymous Christian artist should show Christ and Judas together in this way. I expect the artist's intention was to play on the contrast between the Godlike Christ and the sinful suicide who has got his come-uppance. After all, the biblical texts all condemn Judas. He is reviled in Christian piety as the worst of men. The poet Dante consigned him to the lowest circle of hell. Yet I found it impossible to read the carving in this way. I couldn't help but feel a sympathy for the hanged man. He seemed peaceful in his death. His face is turned half to Christ and half to heaven. The two figures seem to know each other, as though dying has united them. Judas and Jesus, Jesus and Judas. Victim and traitor and somehow twins.

There was a freshness about this ancient image which cut across my expectations. This Christ is stronger than death, stronger than sin. He does not appeal for our sympathy, but even in death is labouring with those whose hurts and deaths are worse than his own, simply because they are so utterly hopeless and squalid. These too, the carving seems to say, he owns, he embraces, they are part of his Passion. Judas is not abandoned but comforted.

I went away – perhaps the crowds did too – having seen salvation in a different way, a way which might make new sense of why we call this Friday Good.

VESUVIUS:
OUR PAGAN ROOTS

9 August 2000

I've just come back from southern Italy, where I visited Mount Vesuvius, the only live volcano on the European mainland. Peering into the crater I fancied I saw steam, and perhaps I did – it's fifty-six years since the last eruption and apparently things are hotting up again.

At the foot of the mountain lie the ruins of the Roman town, Herculaneum. Most of the town is still buried in the lava which destroyed it when Vesuvius erupted in AD 79, right at the beginning of the Christian era, before even the Gospels of Matthew and John had been written. It's just been announced that an American electronics company is prepared to fund new excavations, and scholars hope to find the ancient library which could turn out to be a treasure house, containing classical works known about but lost for two thousand years.

Archaeologists have recently found hundreds of skeletons, crushed into the ancient harbour. People were running to the sea when they were engulfed by a wave of lava moving at two hundred miles an hour. The skeletons are perfectly preserved, the teeth still visible, indicating people clutching each other, burying their faces as doom approached. You can still see fragments of charred wood, even fabrics and stores of grain, as everyday life in a fairly prosperous Roman town slid to its catastrophic end.

It's a poignant reminder of our European roots; that we were indeed once children of the Roman empire. The architecture of Herculaneum was replicated from the Grampians to north Africa. There was a common way of life, town planning, good roads, fast food, temples and cults to suit every taste, a whole social world based on privilege and supported by commerce and slavery. At the pinnacle of power was the emperor, who was a kind of earthly God, holding everything together.

Our roots are here, but I found myself reminded that the primitive Christian community said a firm and decisive 'No' to much of the grandeur that was Rome. They hated the injustice that supported such splendour, the wealth and corruption, the sexual licence, the cruel public spectacles. They owed no loyalty to a world that they believed would pass away. The fire of the volcano was as nothing compared to the day when all the world would be consumed in fire, and God would be Lord of all. Ironically, it was other-worldly Christianity which took over the great empire; sapped its pagan spirit and yet preserved what it overcame.

We inherit the public life of the empire with its civil religion, its blend of bureaucracy and cynicism. But there is also the rebel streak of primitive Christianity, eccentric, private and potentially subversive, with its belief in a God who refuses to be identified with any state or institution. Both are part of the soul of Europe and perhaps we need to excavate that past to secure our spiritual future.

THE TSAR AND THE SUBMARINERS

16 August 2000

It's probably little comfort to those one hundred and sixteen still trapped in their submarine under the Barents Sea that the last emperor of Russia has just been declared a saint by the bishops of the Russian Orthodox Church.

Nicholas II and his family were shot dead by their Bolshevik enemies in the summer of 1918. The last of the Tsars has never been seen as much of a hero. He led his country into a disastrous war in the Far East in which the whole of the Russian fleet was sunk. When people rioted in St Petersburg he told the authorities to shoot them. He finally abdicated under pressure, no doubt hoping to save himself and his family, and so paved the way for Lenin's October Revolution and seventy years of Communism.

The Russian Church is responding to a wave of fascination with Nicholas; he's becoming a cult figure. The bishops say he and his family are worthy of sainthood because they were passion-bearers, martyrs, they accepted death with Christian humility. It's not unknown to canonize an inadequate monarch; our own Charles the First is celebrated as a martyr, not least for the dignity with which he went to the scaffold. But murdered monarchs leave unhealed wounds, stirring a potent mix of guilt and devotion. Our Roundhead Revolution was followed remarkably quickly by the restoration of the *status quo*. But the unhealed legacy of the Russian revolution still scars the soul of Russia and endangers the world.

President Putin hopes to restore the Russian Navy as a global force. Yet nuclear vessels are decaying in their docks, the reactors and warheads corroding into instability. We've heard of dozens of accidents on other submarines, of servicemen unpaid and demoralized, of officials selling dangerous equipment to the highest bidder. Even the latest naval vessels are high tech, but low on any kind of imaginative design for human comfort. Communism lived on a dream of power in which people were, in the end, mere functionaries of the great vision. It has left an environmental and social wasteland.

The Russian Church will not help if its motive in making Nicholas a saint is to try to evoke a lost imperial dream. But there might be another reason why this canonization is timely. Russian memories still have to be healed. The bleak, atheist ideology allowed lives to be swallowed up and forgotten, names to disappear, the dead to have no resting place. In the absence of God there was little room for human dignity. There were millions who suffered like Nicholas and his family during the seventy years of Communism.

If his martyrdom can embrace and represent all those known and unknown (and that must include those who have died in the Barents Sea) then perhaps some hope of a more human future can be salvaged from his (and their) death.

BIG BROTHER:
MORE THAN MEETS THE EYE

23 August 2000

Whenever I was miserable as a child I used to think that I would feel better if I knew there was someone watching over me all the time. I thought that's what God did. If there's someone who can see me, who can watch me, then I must really exist. This sounds rather philosophical, but I think in my case it had more to do with being short-sighted. I remember one summer feeling trapped and isolated because the trees were all out of focus. Because I couldn't see, I somehow thought I couldn't be seen.

I've been watching *Big Brother* in the hope of seeing something revealed about what we are really like. The hope is all, of course. It is strangely flattering having a role as watchers. We can be benign or critical. We can vote for people to disappear. This is surely like being God. What it also shows is that being watched is not a comforting experience. There is real anxiety in *Big Brother*'s household. Layers of it are in the body language; it is peeled off in intense conversations and stony silences; its depths exposed to the unblinking eye of the camera.

You begin to get the impression that the participants only know themselves in what they reveal and in what is mirrored back to them. The observing psychiatrists know the truth that they don't know themselves. And perhaps this is the point. It's almost a cliché of today that all is surface, and there is no depth. Life is style without substance. We are what we seem.

As I grew, I slowly developed a sense of myself. That is, I found ways of asking myself what I was thinking and feeling. I didn't need to share these things with anyone, though sometimes I longed to and sometimes I did. Becoming a person was linked to this trust in my own inner life. I realize now that all spirituality begins with introspection, and it is inside the true self that one finds the true God. That's why in an unbelieving world we are driven to find external proofs of ourselves: mirrors, shrinks, lenses, intimate others who, we fondly hope, will tell us who we are. But how can they if we don't already know?

It's wonderfully ironic that of all the characters on *Big Brother* it is only Nasty Nick who has revealed an inner life. He got thrown out for breaking the rules, for keeping something back. But Nick always acted as one who knew that the all-seeing eye is actually quite blind. Beastly though he was, he knew the one ancient truth, which television distorts but cannot destroy: there is more to him than meets the eye. As there is, thank God, to all of us.

PANIC-PRONE SOCIETY

30 August 2000

I was at the deli counter at Sainsbury's yesterday, about to buy some ham for a lunch-time sandwich, when the nightmare started. Images of invisible prions lurking over the meat counter, bringing contamination, madness and death to every slice. Not only beef, but pork and poultry are now suspected of carrying BSE.

Whether the new fears are justified or not, I was struck by how quickly my mind had tuned itself to panic mode. I went home with my packet of ham and a newspaper – defiant, and yet unable to dislodge the mental pictures of staggering cows and burning carcasses. I think we've become a panic-prone society – which is odd, considering how little of real substance we have to panic about. South Africa faces millions of deaths in an AIDS epidemic which is still officially denied, but we seem to live in the confident expectation of a major public health disaster. BSE today, GM monsters tomorrow.

Panic is very near the surface, and – this is a confession – though I believe in God, I am temperamentally a panicker. Not only about big things like BSE, but about trivial frustrations which happen every day. Panic hits me when I'm in a queue and someone in front of me dithers, forever changing their mind or losing their change. My blood pressure goes up in traffic jams – and lifts. Once when a car blocked me in on a Sunday on my way to church I had to struggle not to scratch my revenge in its paint-work with my car keys. I think it was only the panic that I might be seen in clerical clothes performing this act that stopped me. There's something in the atmosphere which generates panic, or perhaps it's in the water. Anyway, I'm sure its ultimate cause is spiritual.

If I examine the feelings that go with panic, the anxiety and rage and helplessness – it seems to be a fear of losing control. Why do we fear, we who have so much? I think the reason is that we don't trust our luck, we think it must run out. Our prosperity makes us insecure. We cling to what we have, terrified that it will be taken away.

This makes everyone permanently jumpy and aggressive – and it's not wise. We would do better to cultivate trust, not blind trust; but belief in what used to be called Providence. Providence isn't feeling smug because God has apparently provided for you and not for others. It is a confidence to accept the way the universe is, even in the face of potential disaster. It encourages not panic, but gratitude and generosity. It doesn't invite the worst but knows it could happen. Even then it struggles to maintain perspective. It was the disaster-prone Job who was eventually able to say of God: 'Though he slay me, yet will I trust in him.'

CITIZENSHIP

13 December 2000

The new school textbook on citizenship, launched today, has already attracted plenty of flak. Critics complain that it is yet one more subject for the overstretched curriculum. They sneer at its talk of lifelong personal development and caring, sharing values. And yes, I have to admit my heart sank rather, as early reports of its contents evoked images of ranks of smiling workers singing anthems in praise of the company or the State. I suppose it's because I'm English and C. of E. and prefer things like values to be implicit and understated rather than lit up with key words and handed on in embarrassing group exercises.

And yet I feel I should squash my scepticism and be pleased. And I am in a way. For the first time for ages here is a resource for schools which is not afraid to use the language of the spirit. It is as though it has suddenly become obvious that education can't be done in a vacuum of values; that schools play a part in forming people; and that means, to use traditional language, making souls.

But then my doubts take a different turn. I was brought up in the years after the 1944 Education Act which compelled schools to provide religious instruction and worship at morning assembly. Every school day from the age of five to eighteen I sang a hymn, listened to verses from the Bible and said at least one prayer. At the time, everyone thought that this was the way to make children Christian. The best way to ensure good citizenship was to give children a hefty dose of religion in their school years. At my school, provision was made for Jews and Catholics, later Muslims, to have their own prayers. People thought it didn't really matter if the children ended up as believers or not, at least they'd be good. So the argument went – but it was wrong. Children did get a hearty dose of Christianity, and it was enough to make them immune. It didn't *take* because spiritual values need to be lived, not talked about. Most schools were not in any real sense Christian communities, most parents wanted the values but not necessarily the faith. Their children ended up with neither.

There's no point in learning about spirituality if the school itself is a wholly secular institution, where the real values are competitive and materialistic. If staff are only interested in exam results, souls won't grow. Virtue needs time to take root and flower. If teachers are hopelessly stressed, how can they live the message of good citizenship, which is all about respect, patience and courtesy. Everyone knows that concerned presence in the classroom is worth more than a million words. A textbook can explore and explain what we believe to be true, but it can't create it. Only we can do that.

GOD AT BOTH ENDS OF THE ARGUMENT

20 December 2000

Yesterday Parliament debated whether there should be research on cloned human embryos. It was in essence a theological debate, though without the religious vocabulary, which we've lost in public. Though, God knows, I meet it all the time in private.

So let me put the God word back, and let me speak on both sides of the argument. The first 'me' believes deeply in the sacredness of human life. Every newborn baby renews my faith in God. From a mere sliver of human tissue a unique individual has emerged, body and soul, God's very image and likeness. Perhaps the soul is infused at conception, perhaps it develops through time. But there is no point early enough in the process for me to be sure that this bundle of cells is not spun direct from God's sacred web. And even if the cells are not sacred, I must treat them as so, because if I fail to I will cease to see the image of God at other points of human vulnerability: when a foetus is unwanted, when people get old and ill. So the first 'me' draws the line here; no cloned embryos, no stem cell research. The cost is too high, the risk is too great. Such meddling is a blasphemy not only against life, but against the creator of all life.

But then the second 'me' is the parent of a daughter who is dying. Her disease comes from a faulty gene which could have been replaced. She has had only half a life and soon she will lose that. There are thousands like her, millions the world over. Her condition makes me angry with the perfect God who forbids us to question his handiwork. Why, when others are born well, did he foul up in her case? But perhaps God is compassionate, perhaps God suffers with us. Perhaps he is revealing the mysteries of creation through science, so that he can inspire us to heal what is broken in this world. Such a God would rather we tried and got it wrong than that we did nothing in the face of pain. So, a cautious green light to stem cell research. The cost can be measured, the risks can be limited. Not to try would be a culpable refusal to use our gifts for God's glory and humanity's good.

So the first 'me' and second 'me' talk to each other, and their thoughts were reflected yesterday in the speeches of those who can no longer speak of God. It is a pity we have lost the right language for this debate, for without God the two sides have nothing in common. But with God at both ends of the argument the two 'me's may at least stumble their way towards common ground.

NEW YEAR, NEW SPROUTS

3 January 2001

It must be the most controversial advertising campaign of the winter, stirring stormier passions than even the recent perfume ad of Sophie Dahl in her high heels and diamonds. I'm referring of course to Thomas Cook's arrestingly plain dish of green sprouts and the message about it being time to get away.

Is it a brutal attack on sprouts? This was my first thought, and I was incensed. To defend the honour of the sprout I bought a whole branch of sprouts – a sprout tree – as a protest. It seems so unkind to attack sprouts when they have been trying to make their image more British by dropping the 'Brussels'. The man from Thomas Cook who tried to soften the blow by saying that the ad really meant it was all right to go on holiday because you've eaten your sprouts was being disingenuous. The sprouts have not been touched but lie forever cold on their ice-white plate. These are unloved sprouts.

But perhaps they're symbolic sprouts? Do they represent an attack on the EC, with Brussels at its heart? Leave Europe to winter and brassicas, and head for the sun. Or perhaps the campaign is a subtle critique of the family Christmas? The little dish of sprouts, so together, yet so forlorn, unable to escape the plate, their individuality merged in a green mass identity? Or is it just a rather rude reference to sprouts as possible producers of wind? Get away from post-Christmas digestive disorders by uprooting to an exotic location. You won't be offered sprouts on your paradise beach.

It's not surprising that the sprout should have inspired such a brilliant assault. They are eternally comic vegetables; even their fans find it difficult to find them a place in the temples of haute cuisine. Yet the irony is that sprouts are probably the healthiest part of the Yuletide feast. Lots of Vitamin C, iron, fibre and folic acid. All the New Year diets boil down to eating up your greens, and cutting back on wicked sugar and fat.

In the secular calendar the season of fasting has been brought forward from Lent to 2 January and why not get over your New Year hangovers with a cold dish of sprouts? Cheaper than a holiday, the humble sprout reminds us whereof we are made. Of the earth, earthy, dust from dust. The greenness is our invest-ment in life and vitality. Not only of the body but of the spirit too. For the greenness of the holly and the ivy and the Christmas tree itself represents the life that doesn't die, green being a mystical symbol for divinity. *Verditas*, the sacred freshness, deep-down things. Though the years pass and the seasons change and our bodies wear out and our minds decay, the waters of divinity still bubble up like a spring, chuckling at our human vanity, welling up to eternal life.

DESTROYING IMAGES

9 March 2001

I remember as a child being taken on a family outing to the cathedral at Ely and being fascinated by the Lady Chapel which was as bright and pretty as a wedding cake. Plain glass, crisp white stone with mysterious arches and crevices. Much later I realized that the prettiness is an illusion. The chapel is a grave-yard. During the age of Cromwell, religious extremists hacked off the heads of the carved saints and angels leaving ragged, empty space. Today, as you look at the stumps that remain, you're left wondering what great hate could inspire such a frenzied attack. What was so dangerous about this sacred art? The question's in my mind today as the Taliban of Afghanistan prepare to blow up two massive statues of the Buddha that have stood in the hills for fifteen hundred years.

I think Cromwell's men thought that the Ely carvings were

what the second commandment calls graven images, obstacles to the worship of the true God. They feared that they caused superstition and idolatry – spiritual infections which would bring down God's wrath. By destroying them, they meant to establish purity. They must have believed that God approved, that he hated the statues as much as they did. After all, the Bible says that God is a jealous God.

The Taliban authorities want to disinfect the landscape of its Buddhist past. No doubt they also believe that they are fulfilling God's will.

The curious thing is that both the puritans of the seventeenth century and the militants of Taliban seem to impute more power to the images they want to obliterate than those who value them. The stone Buddhas were not built to be worshipped – there is no worship as such in Buddhism; they were built to inspire people. The calm image of compassion landscaped into the cliff was a gigantic focus for the eye, but it also fed the spirit, reminding people that the purpose of life is wisdom and kindness.

But the purists of Taliban are gripped by the fear that the carved Buddhas are so strong and dangerous as to be rivals to God. Of course this fear can never be admitted. The Taliban leader has claimed disingenuously that 'all we are breaking is stones'. All? Is that why they crave a faceless landscape purged of reminders of its ancient faith?

I am coming to realize that the tragedy of iconoclasts is that they are so often secret idolaters. It is only because they impute such hideous strength to images that they are compelled to destroy them. Perhaps the most dangerous idol is the one that has no form at all, that exists in the mind of those who wipe out what is sacred to others.

SURRENDERED WIFE

23 March 2001

'A surrendered wife knows how to be vulnerable, trusting, respectful and grateful . . . in marriage as in ballroom dancing, one must lead and the other must follow . . .' That's from a new American best-seller by Laura Doyle, *The Surrendered Wife*. Surrender means 'Stop trying to control your husband. Honour his choice of socks. Pool your money, let him control it, cut up your credit cards, you'll never know how generous he is until you let go of the family finances . . .' By now you'll have got the picture and you'll either be cheering or boiling with rage.

One thoughtful reaction to *The Surrendered Wife* was from a husband who acknowledged that yes, his wife had, indeed surrendered to him on their wedding day. But then, he said, 'On our wedding day I also surrendered to her.' I was touched and then shocked. It's the word 'surrender'. In our me-first society it sounds like the ultimate defeat. Who wants to come out with a white flag and give themselves up? Surely the secular gospel of self-affirmation makes a virtue of us getting our way, and condemns giving in as cowardice.

Laura Doyle has touched a raw nerve. If no one gives in, there's domestic misery and she sees that in nagging wives, sullen husbands and dysfunctional families. Her answer, though, is only half an answer. One-sided surrender is a recipe for tyranny; the false peace that comes where one controls and one submits.

Perhaps the truth is that it takes two defeats to make a marital victory. At least that seems to be implied in the Marriage Service. In its modern form, bride and groom say to one another: 'All that I am I give to you, and all that I have I share with you . . .' And what that means is very drastic; it is a mutual and total surrender of possessions and power – a mutual and total surrender of the self.

Christians are always going on about self-giving, but the word 'surrender' is stronger than that. Self-giving implies a degree of control; I give myself and I can still take back what I give. But surrender is total. It is a play with the imagery of war that is as inspiring as it is potentially offensive. I rather like the idea of marriage as the place where the age-long battle of the sexes comes to an end in mutual defeat.

Because in the end, to be defeated by love is also what most of us long for, to find that there is someone so much more important to me than me, that I would lay down my life for them.

The Marriage Service likens this mutual surrender to the heart of the Christian mystery. Human salvation depends on another surrender, of Christ laying down his life in surrender to the Father's will, and of our laying down our lives in response. No winners or losers then, in this game of death and love.

FAITH COMMUNITIES

28 March 2001

Tony Blair spent part of yesterday addressing Christian socialists as part of his mission to various 'faith communities'. William Hague has also taken an interest in religious groups in recent months. I know I ought to be pleased about this, flattered that our leaders are apparently targeting people like me. But I'm not. I don't mind politicians angling for my vote, but I don't want to be wooed just because I go to church. Their strategy assumes something about communities of faith which I think is wrong. And that is that they exist as special interest groups, like vegetarians or sports fanatics. But that's not true, especially of the largest of our so-called faith communities, the Christian Church.

So why are they doing it? Tony Blair deplores the cynicism

people have towards politicians, and yet I can't help wondering whether he and others are appealing to faith groups as a renewable source of useful do-gooders, whose philanthropy can be enlisted to make up the gaps in various kinds of State provision. And if that's so, then I hope they're wrong. Churches are not there to get people to do good, they are there to help people worship God. They can do their bit to promote virtue, though most Christians I know struggle rather than succeed to live half-decent lives, and even then, they can't do virtue for everyone else.

The one thing that faith communities do have is a reach into society that politicians envy. Church people usually know, by a strange process of gossip, prayer and osmosis, what is going on in the wider community. It's just because of that that it's wrong to treat them simply as well-meaning voluntary organizations which people choose to sign up to or shun. Sort of pigeon-fanciers for God, significant minorities who have to be either courted or appeased. If they are like that, then they deserve the nervous criticism voiced by some secular agencies this week, that faith-inspired social projects are likely to be divisive.

The whole point of churches is that they are not really communities at all. They are at best loose networks of individuals and families who join and separate and move on and back in increasingly complex ways. Churches are full of lonely people looking for friends, and gregarious people looking for action and quite ordinary people looking for inspiration, and people who want to be private and alone with God. The New Testament model for the Church is not a gathered lump sitting together with the doors shut waiting for the prime minister to call by, but salt. Tiny grains of sharpness and disinfectant scattered over a much wider community. Rather horrid on its own. But when you shake it out it sure flavours the crisps.

ANNUAL REPORT?

6 April 2001

Here is an item from this week's news which never made it into the bulletins. Following the report of the Department of Trade and Industry into the Maxwell pensions scandal, representatives of the leading law, banking and accountancy firms, government ministers and former members of the board of the *Mirror* group who were criticized in the report issued the following corporate confession:

> We confess that we have sinned in taking profit for our god and bowing down and worshipping it before all other gods. We confess that we have made to ourselves a graven image of smooth success in which more is always better than enough and honesty is a virtue we cannot afford. We confess that we are shocked and very sorry for Robert Maxwell's pensioners but what could we do about them? It was their fault for working for him.
>
> We acknowledge that the consequences of his dishonesty have passed on into the next generation who said they were very sorry.
>
> We confess that our former reputation for probity is in tatters; our regulatory mechanisms and our monitoring systems all turned out to be useless.
>
> We have kept holy all trading days and nights, we have worshipped the Nikkei, the FTSE and the Dow Jones and most of us have done rather well.
>
> We have not honoured what our fathers and mothers taught us about right and wrong, but they were naïve for today's complex economy and nobody has found out how to put morality back into the market place when there are fortunes to be made.

We have done no murder and no more than the usual amount of adultery.

But we acknowledge that we smoothed the way for dishonesty, fraud and theft to the tune of £460 million.

We have protested our innocence, our ignorance and now that we have been named all we have left to confess is our incompetence. Because, you see, we thought Maxwell for all his faults had a charmed life and would always deliver the goods.

And we coveted our £2 million mansion in the home counties, our pads in the city, two cars, three holidays a year, private health insurance and all other requirements of an average, decent life.

And there is no health in us or in our institutions or in the financial industry which allowed all this to happen.

Since this confession has not actually been made, it is difficult for us to imagine suitable penance or to give any kind of secular absolution. One of the virtues of capitalism is that it knows it needs a morality. It is not built in and can never be taken for granted. It's a marvellous tool for making money multiply, but without a strong ethic it brings all of us to ruin. The DTI said ethics must be put back into the heart of business practice. So perhaps a suitable penance would be for some of those named and shamed to tell us their personal rule of life for ensuring that they and we are not deceived again.

THE CROSS

Boris Becker has confessed this week what a heavy price he has paid for his brief encounter in a broom cupboard with the Russian model Angela Ermakova. I guess his contrition has divided the public in two, with half feeling sorry for the star, whose golden glamour is now so tarnished, and half cheering that he got what he deserved.

We humans are a fairly opinionated lot, ever ready to label public figures as guilty or innocent according to our own prejudices. Becker's either a nice lad ruined by a vamp or a Neanderthal blaming the female of the species for his downfall in the tradition of the Garden of Eden. We've been here before with Bill Clinton and Monica Lewinsky; the brevity and silliness of the act in question makes the argument about it all the more compelling. Throwing our moral stones against one or other of the perpetrators is like pass the parcel: whoever is left holding on to the blame is out. The blame game is so fascinating that we are tempted to play it in all our important relationships. You know the sort of thing. You hurt me. I'll get my own back. You make me feel guilty. It's all your fault. It's all my fault – until everything ends predictably in tears and compensation.

It's tempting to want God – if there is a God – to sit above it all like the ultimate moral referee, parcelling out the guilt and declaring the punishments. Both sides can appeal of course, and both often do, and usually the outcome is an uneasy draw.

Good Friday stirs in our memory the image of the innocent, crucified Christ. The wounds and the nails communicate to some the depths of divine love, to others, human barbarity. When the eccentric genius Salvador Dali painted the cross he had a different angle altogether. His cross hung steeply above the turning world, his crucified Christ looks down on the earth in the majesty of distance. The cross is huge, the earth small, as though the cross questions both our blaming and our excusing. Dali's cross is like God's throne towering over space and all the centuries, guarding the fragile earth, absorbing guilt and blame and weakness and suffering and hurt. If there is judgement, it is in its silent strength which makes us quiet too. Before this cross no one is innocent. And no one is condemned. The cross is the price tag paid by the creator for having dreamed up a universe with people in it as complicated as we are.

I think that's why on this secular Good Friday with the shops open and the holiday traffic on the move there are still significant numbers of people who will find their way to church to reflect on the cross and the words of the crucified Christ: 'Father, forgive them, for they know not what they do . . .'

GREATER THAN
A MILLION HANDBAGS

20 April 2001

I can't get Elizabeth Sherlock out of my mind this week. Her picture's been everywhere and so has a public sense of shock at her horrible death after her handbag was pinched at Euston Station.

We've all got nervous recently of criminal behaviour in public places. I've seen handbag thefts, and I know how you do it, at least on the London Tube. You jump in one door and out the next. No one can catch you if you time it right between stops, and you rely on the fact that the vast majority of passengers will be hiding behind their newspapers, determined not to get involved.

I once witnessed racial bullying on a bus and was excruciatingly embarrassed. I was rooted, tongue-tied to my seat, pathetically grateful for the brave teenager who quietened the bully and comforted the victim, but aware of how tense and frightened everyone had become. As though we had no idea what to do or think or say. Most of us deplore casual robberies and abusive incidents in public places. Yet we sit silent like the three monkeys: see no evil, hear no evil, speak no evil, hoping our passivity will make the evil go away. Which it does until the next time.

Inside this fear is a real lack of faith in the sovereignty of the good. We really believe that evil is stronger than goodness, more powerful, more effective, perhaps even more attractive. We blame the police, drugs, schools, the media, the breakdown of the family, but the real problem is within us: our lack of morale, our too easy acceptance that we can do nothing. Our helplessness is quickly picked up by the desperate and immoral who become more and more contemptuous of civilized conduct. We have got ourselves into a vicious circle, and the root of it is spiritual.

We have come to believe that good behaviour is only a private choice and that we shouldn't impose our personal codes on others. So rudeness, rage and threatening talk fill the spaces we have vacated, making an atmosphere in which we almost expect people to behave badly.

In this Easter Week the Christian Church is celebrating the victory of the cross. The triumph of good over evil, life over death. Every Easter hymn is full of alleluias. There is a note of joy and resolution that life is worth living because One came back from the dead.

Once we knew that our common life depended on what Easter represents, the sheer beauty and invincibility of the Good. How did we lose our confidence? Who has stolen it from us? And can it be resurrected? For its loss is greater than a million handbags; it is eroding our very humanity.

WHAT DOES ROSIE THINK?

18 June 2001

We've all been made to think by the case of the conjoined twins who were attached in such a way that only one had a chance of survival. And now at last we've seen Gracie Attard, a bright little girl with her mother's brown eyes and an unmistakable look of mischief. Ten months ago her chances were slim. Quite apart from her desperate condition there was the view of her parents and most church leaders that it was immoral to try to save 'Jodie' as she was then called, at the expense of her twin, Rosie, officially called Mary.

As August moved to September and the dilemma moved to the courts I found myself less and less convinced by the case that the Church was making. It seemed to me to be too absolute, too black and white. I found myself drawn to the more obviously humanist argument that one life is better than none. Yet that, too, in the end, seemed heartless. I probably wasn't the only one who was both surprised, troubled and relieved by the judgement of the court which allowed the operation to go ahead. My conscience was still uneasy.

Then I went to a conference which had nothing to do with hard ethical questions. But the case was very much on people's minds and so it was hardly surprising that when a Christian ethical expert gave a paper on another subject, members of the audience asked his opinion on the fate of the twins. So he did, tentatively, offer his thoughts. He made it clear that he saw the strength of the traditional Christian view. And yet in this case it did not satisfy him.

I felt he shared my fear that it was, like the humanist argument, too rational. The dimension of feeling seemed to be missing from both sides. Then he invited us all to imagine what Rosie, or Mary as she was known at the time, what Rosie would have wanted. Supposing it were possible for Mary to know both that her own life could not last and also that she, alone could give Jodie a chance of life. Would she not have wanted her sister to live?

I knew, of course, that in traditional Christian morality this exercise in imagination would be illegitimate, the point would be made against it that Mary – Rosie – couldn't make that decision for herself. But, pressed the speaker, how do we know we can't make that decision for her, with her?

I felt that these questions probed the issue more sensitively than either the traditional religious argument or the utilitarian one. I found myself thinking that if Rosie could be thought of as a person in her own right, then she was made in the image of a God whose very nature is self-sacrifice. Was it so wrong to assume that she would want life for Gracie? Or should we conclude that selves are utterly selfish, and that Rosie would have envied her sister's chance so much as to prefer her to perish?

I can't help hoping now that, wherever she is, Rosie is glad that her sister is alive.

PUBLIC OR PRIVATE

26 June 2001

Once, we all knew that our public services were the product of virtue. Whatever their inefficiencies, they were the fruit of a great idea. Equal access for everyone to health, education and all the necessities of contemporary life. Then we learnt that the public services were not virtuous at all. They gobbled taxes, wasted resources and didn't deliver. So private became virtuous instead. We were told that the hungry tigers of enterprise would give choice and accountability, cut out waste and flatten bureaucracy. But after some years of this new orthodoxy and a few notorious disasters, the enthusiasm for privatizing everything has died.

Now the government's got the big idea of partnership, the best of private and public working together. Already it's under attack, from unions, think-tanks and disgruntled MPs because nobody knows what partnership really means. A partnership is a shared enterprise. Partners are equal but they do different things. It should mean deciding which bits of our public services are run more effectively for profit and which bits really work better if they are publicly funded.

It's this thinking which still needs to be done. Some obvious ways of bringing in private services turn out to be ineffective. Think of the way the cleaning, the laundry, the catering, the maintenance get contracted out to private firms. Managers congratulate themselves on saving money. Everything should be satisfactory, but it often isn't.

Why? Because the little jobs, the dirty, repetitive, uninteresting jobs turn out to be the nuts and bolts which enable the whole machine to work. We tend to value the people with the cerebral skills, but they are helpless without stable support which has a bit of slack in the system. How often in a hospital you see busy consultants steaming past filthy waste bins, gleaming and glamorous operating theatres with non-acute wards full of dirty laundry. Morale suffers, everyone gets ratty and feels uncared for. If the little jobs aren't resourced generously the whole system eventually breaks down. One of the most telling metaphors of a human organization is that of a human body, head, limbs, muscles, nerves all working in a co-ordinated way. It was St Paul's most famous metaphor for the Christian Church. He knew that there are bits of the organism which flourish best if they're relatively free, and other bits which work best if they're well protected.

What private enterprise can supply is the drive and imagination that reaches out for the future, thrives on competition, fights for every penny, and takes risks. Is it too much to hope that old-fashioned morality and hard-headed efficiency could come together in public–private partnerships? That the necessary risks of enterprise could be borne by those with most to give, not most to lose?

USES OF DRUGS

2 July 2001

We've got ourselves into a bit of a muddle about soft drugs. After the policy of zero tolerance, there's a trial scheme just started in Lambeth to let cannabis smokers off with a mere caution. I've always felt rather hypocritical about soft drugs, nervous of those I've never tried (like pot), but quite at ease with the ones I like. In fact, if ten in the morning comes without my habitual dose of caffeine I start to fantasize about double espressos. Later, the chime of six brings a pleasant anticipation of a cool glass of Chardonnay. I can give respectable reasons for my mild addictions. Wine is good for health in moderation – it's also in the Bible as a gift of God 'to gladden the human heart' as Psalm 104 puts it.

Yet the line between use and abuse is a thin one. I know, like Bridget Jones, the dreadful sensation of bits of machinery and pheasants in the head that indicate I overdid it. We human beings get addicted easily to substances which make us feel relaxed, attentive, cheerful, calm. That's because those feelings are akin to spiritual experience. I once read a book by a monk who had worked with recovering alcoholics and come to the conclusion that in every drinker's thirst was a longing for God. I was sceptical about this until I remembered that many religions speak of God as being happy, blissful, blessed; as though that expansive, generous glow which a drug can induce really does mirror something about ultimate reality. If this is true, then perhaps there is in God something like a festival going on where the food and the wine never run out and the pleasure does not pall.

We are attracted to pleasure, why shouldn't we be? But we can't enjoy total pleasure for very long. Human brains and bodies just can't manage it. Those natural substances which make us feel good in moderation destroy our minds and livers in excess. We have to train ourselves for the right use of pleasure.

That's exactly what we've done with the drugs we've domesticated. Perhaps we now have a chance to civilize cannabis, to see if it can serve a good purpose. It's worth asking what drugs are for. At least some of the soft drugs that nature provides – and I am thinking of my six o'clock appointment with a glass, perhaps it will be Sauvignon tonight – ease the pain and stress of the day, and remind us that we are more than machines.

Within us is the image of a God who labours over creation but then rests and celebrates on the seventh day. Conviviality and relaxation are not only good for us. They are anticipations of the heaven for which we are created – that end, which is no end.

BENEDICT AND ISLAM

10 July 2001

When the Bradford riots broke out last Saturday I was in a convent in South Wales discussing the civilizing effect of the *Rule of St Benedict*. This short book of rules on how to be a community of monks was written fifteen hundred years ago. It has probably had more influence on Western Europe than any other book apart from the Bible. Though it was meant for enclosed monks, Anglicans have taken their daily prayers from Benedict, Quakers their silence, Puritans their industry; and that's even without counting the Catholics who started it all. Even today, dotted round the country, are schools and abbeys and convents where men and women still try to live a common life according to Benedict's *Rule*.

So I came back to news of the riots. As I crossed the Severn Bridge back from the retreat I found myself thinking that the fundamental teachings of Islam have much in common with those of Benedict. They even share a similar origin, in the deserts of the Middle East, where the first Christian monks and the first Muslim communities tried to find ways of living according to God's will. Islam means submission to God; Benedict teaches obedience to God. Both insist on humility. Both try to create communities that are kind as well as fair. Both teach the importance of good manners, courtesy, helpfulness and self-control. Neither is afraid of discipline, punishment. The sight of Muslims prostrating themselves at prayer is not so different from that of black-robed Benedictines filing into church, the call to prayer from the minaret is not so different from the haunting plainsong of the Benedictine abbey.

People were saying yesterday that the Bradford riots were not about race or religion. They were caused by angry and alienated young men who have been deprived of any civilizing vision. For years politicians, schools and the media have made the fatal assumption that religion was divisive and not to be trusted. They have assumed that only secular values could mediate between different cultures, that respect would flourish best in a Godless vacuum. Yet this is simply untrue. If only material values count, respect goes by the board, and our inner cities become breeding grounds of envy seeking a target. As one commentator said drily yesterday, 'It wasn't the boys who go to the mosque who were throwing stones at the police.' But those Asian youths who did were surely imitating the despair they have learnt from their once Christian counterparts. For years we've treated churchgoing and religious instruction as though they had nothing to do with anything that mattered. 'Listen, my Son . . .' begins the *Rule of St Benedict* – and we would do well to listen. If we want peace on our streets, the peace Islam and Benedict both commend, we need to dig a lot deeper into our spiritual heritage.

RUSSIAN CONTRADICTIONS

28 August 2001

What we hear from Russia today usually comes in the form of a list of awful problems – social, economic, political. I've just got back from a cruise round the Black Sea which took me to Russia, Turkey, the new republic of the Ukraine and the once satellite state of Bulgaria. I've been tossed about in the currents of the Bosporus and scorched in the Dardanelles. I've stood in the very room in Yalta where Stalin, Roosevelt and Churchill carved up the world after the Second World War. I've seen where the Light Brigade charged into the Valley of Death. I've visited cathedrals that have come alive after years of neglect. And all the time I've felt the weight of history: the empires Byzantine, Seljuk, Ottoman, Soviet; the religions of Orthodoxy and Islam; and the endless movements of people seeking new homes, establishing borders, going to war over land and faith and driving out minorities.

So what happens now to Russia and its former friends? The Russia I visited was no longer the heart of the Soviet empire, but a nation looking for its soul. We saw the sunny coast where high-ranking party members used to spend their summers. It's now littered with villas for the newly rich and glitzy hotels for tourists. We grumbled over the arrival of McDonald's – there was something almost shameful about being greeted in the country of the endless samovar with tea bag, polystyrene and 'Have a nice day'. Of course not everyone regrets the past. It's particularly hard for Russians to accept liberation, since they have lost so much. Their former satellites have the excitement of new nationhood, but Russia has only herself. It's hard to find yourself in competition with former allies, to see the shops and marketplaces flooded with goods that you can't afford, to taste a fear you never expected about your pension and your old age.

Western journalists and politicians often seem to sneer at the problems faced by Russia and the new republics. They persuade us that the break-up of Communism has led only to chaos and corruption. Western firms went in looking for quick profits and many have left, spreading a message of hopelessness. But we see what we choose to see. Underneath the economic struggles there is a longing for renewal. In the Ukraine, we visited the birthplace of the Russian people where Prince Vladimir was baptized and brought his new nation into the Orthodox faith. Last week I met a woman in her seventies whose mother had her children secretly baptized, not even telling her daughter so she should not have to lie. Now she has re-found the faith she was not allowed to have.

Let's hope that in the sufferings of the present lie the seed of real freedom. We need to give these new nations time to find themselves. They have already endured the unendurable. It is our shallowness which grows bored with their struggles.

9/14

14 September 2001

There has been a lot of praying in the last few days and there'll be more today as special services are held at St Paul's Cathedral and in Washington. People need space to be with their feelings before normality can be restored. I've found it rather difficult to pray at all, as though my relationship with God, such as it is, has suddenly gone on to very distant and formal terms. I've read the scriptures and said the Psalms, but there's a darkness, as though the falling towers and choking dust have obscured the face of God. There's a rift in reality, a breakdown of trust. It doesn't help that there seems a strong likelihood that the hijackers were religious, and did their dreadful work in the belief that it was God's will. That's when I begin to wonder whether there isn't something toxic about religion, something which drives otherwise sane people to violence. Then I want to say, as I often do, 'Oh, but that's bad religion, that's fanaticism. Real religion isn't like that.'

But I wonder. In the Bible there is a strong sense of the justice of God. Every human soul is absolutely accountable and comes to judgement. There is a final reckoning when good and evil are finally seen for what they are. The last book of the Bible, the book of Revelation, was almost excluded from the New Testament because it had such a lurid picture of everlasting hell. Revelation is a violent Christian polemic against the Roman Empire, whose mighty armies controlled a world in which Christians were deeply suspect dissidents. No one could easily compare imperial Rome with democratic America, but I guess if the hijackers were motivated by religious faith it was because they believed something like the author of the book of Revelation. They believed that things really were that bad. When the world is so out of joint, only terrible gestures register. Perhaps that's the explanation for how they might have come to believe they were instruments of God in a great destruction which was both symbolic and real.

I can't let religion off the hook about this. The striving for justice is in all religions. It is certainly crucial to Christianity, Judaism and Islam. In atheistic societies judgement is more hidden and impersonal – the gulag, the shot in the back of the head, the calculated starvation of millions who don't count. When there is no God to see, cruelty need have no face, no drama. But the biblical religions speak of a God who has feelings, a God who can be angry. That wrath, that darkness is what I am trying to deal with in my prayers. What's almost impossible is to absorb the fact that there are people who are so desperate, or so furious, that throwing away their lives and killing thousands appears the only rational solution.

HEROD: MONARCH OF THE YEAR

28 December 2001

Here's a candidate for the Monarch of the Year poll. He ruled a small nation surrounded by powerful enemies. His people were difficult to manage, and horribly touchy about religion and race. He clamped down on terrorism and sucked up to the nearest superpower with interests in his region. Once in control he proved a great success. He solved the unemployment problem by embarking on a massive problem of public works. He knocked down half a hill for one construction and built an astonishing fortress on top of another. He reigned for thirty-six years, finally dying just after the birth of Christ.

So what verdict is to be passed on Herod the Great? By all the normal criteria he was a good king who advanced the prosperity of his people and protected their independence. But he is better known for an act of spectacular brutality which is reported in Matthew's Gospel, and commemorated in the Christian calendar today: the slaughter of the Holy Innocents. This, we are told, was his response to the news that a child had been born who would bear his title: King of the Jews.

I expect if we had a chance to interview King Herod we would find him rather impressive. Strong and handsome, he would tell us about his cunning diplomacy and his generosity in funding a brand-new temple. If you pressed him about the Holy Innocents he would no doubt say that strong action is justified when security is at stake. In fact security – his own – was the highest item on his personal agenda. Not only the children of Bethlehem but his wife and a fair proportion of his own relations came to a sticky end, as he tried, unsuccessfully, to manage the succession after his death.

Herod the Great was a great man. But that was exactly his problem, as it is for all absolute monarchs, dictators, tribal chieftains, warlords. The more absolute the power, the more total the control, the more vulnerable a leader is. So that in the end, your whole empire and achievement is threatened by little children, who have no real power at all. Herod's massacre of the innocents is a horrid story to end the Christmas festivities with, but it brings us down to earth. The great men can only leave us the past; their palaces, their destructions, victories. But the future lies open and it is from the future that peace calls to us. The real threat to Herod was not another King of Israel but the Prince of Peace, whose challenge is to all who wield power by force and not consent. That's why the Holy Innocents are remembered not only as victims but as martyrs who unknowingly and involuntarily served the cause of God, putting down the mighty from their seat and exalting the humble and meek.

THIS IS MY BODY

4 January 2002

Yesterday we saw pictures of the five little pigs snuffling about in their unashamedly piggy way. In contrast to the images, there was the sinister language which surrounds their creation. These are engineered animals, with turned-off genes, prone to diseases like poor Dolly the sheep. Their Christmassy names will not pacify the anxious, nor disguise the potential profit they represent if cloning can be perfected.

Developments in genetics get to us deeply. It is rather shocking to realize how many of our human genes are identical, not only to pigs, but to unlikely things like fruit flies and even bananas. We are not as special as we think. Perhaps it is because we find we are so close to other species that we are terrified of losing our distinctiveness. Breeding animals as organ donors sounds like cannibalism. Living with a pig's heart pumping my blood around suggests a greater intimacy with pig-ness than eating a bacon sandwich.

What we can't know is what it is like for the pig – how pigs experience the world. We can imagine, of course. This was the charm of the film *Babe* – the story of the pig that learned to be a sheep dog. Before I saw it, a friend swore that I would never eat a sausage again. But she was wrong, because *Babe* was not really about pigs and sheep; it was about competition, cruelty, the triumph of the individual. In real life pigs are not my friends. I want them to be well treated, but I don't send them Christmas cards.

The difference between the human and the non-human is getting harder to define, but there is one characteristic which runs through all nature, and that is that we feed off one another all the time. Humans aren't always dominant. A virus or germ could carry me off. Plants can repair tissue, they eat sunlight and water and nutrients from soil. We live, we die, and dying feeds new life. Some people have always felt squeamish about this and have believed it to be more spiritual to avoid interacting with other species: don't swat flies, don't consume anything which has a face. The Greek genius Pythagoras wouldn't eat broad beans because he thought they had souls.

We either reject the principle of life feeding off life or we find ways to embrace the mystery. There is a principle of sacrifice in nature; the strong and the weak are bound up together and provide each other's needs. As we think about where the limits of science lie, we might remember how shocking is the central Christian ritual, which recalls a God who came to earth to die, and invites us to consume him in the most intimate form: 'This is my Body, this is my Blood.'

GOD PREFERS DIVERSITY

17 January 2002

Today at Lambeth Palace forty scholars – Muslim and Christian – are meeting to look together at the two great faiths. This meeting is important for all of us, for how we deal with 'the other' is the most urgent of our spiritual problems. It affects the secular and the indifferent as well as the committed – even those who have been in the business that the Church calls 'ecumenism' for decades. Religions are enormous, life-shaping things. Being a Christian forms me, informs me, sometimes reforms me and may deform me; and yet the shape of this formation will be quite different than if I were a Muslim.

So how do I meet my different neighbour? I once knew a Catholic historian who was passionate about church unity. What he really wanted was that everyone should become Catholic. He was quite nice about it: he thought Anglican Evensong, Methodist hymns, Baptist preaching, Pentecostal spontaneity and Quaker silences would all fit well into a final united Roman Catholic Church. Then one day he woke up with the unexpected thought that what he really valued most about a friend who was a Baptist was that he was a Baptist. Making a Catholic of him would not be a gain but a loss.

Religion has a bad record. And so, I think, do our agnostic secularists, who would rather like religious people to be neutral, as they think they are – at least in public. History doesn't help. Christian strategy towards Muslims was first to think of them as heretics, then in the Crusades to go to war with them, later to try and convert them. Can we accept the other as other?

Valuable because he or she is not what I am, they show a different facet of humanity. It's much harder than it looks. Yet both Muslims and Christians have resources to cope from their own scriptures. In an article yesterday the Archbishop of Canterbury and Dr Zaki Badawi of the Muslim College referred to the text in the Koran: 'Had God willed he would have made you one community.' They said it implied that God did not want the human race to be one. In the book of Genesis the story of the Tower of Babel shows how God scattered the human race all over the earth and confused our languages, a strong hint that God prefers diversity to unity.

What's going on in Lambeth Palace is more than an opportunity to be friendly. You know – 'It's so nice you're a Muslim. It's so nice you're a Christian', while secretly hoping the other will convert. It is a chance to start working through my desire to turn the other into me, in the hope that I shall reach the moment that I see him as he is and prefer him that way. What begins in respect might lead to love, and what is born of love is born in God.

TWO OLD MEN

16 April 2002

Colin Powell's peace mission is running into the ground. It's not helped by the fact that the battle of wills is being fought by two old men. The old men of the Middle East, who seem curiously alike to me both in their relentlessness and their cunning, are both enormously popular with their frightened peoples. They are trusted for their experience. Everyone knows they won't give an inch more than they have to.

As I've watched them digging themselves into mental bunkers over the past few months, it has occurred to me that there are really good reasons why people over a certain age retire from work. Not only do the old deserve some leisure but, as most of us recognize, there comes a time when experience is worth less than new ideas. We probably overdo the youth bit in Britain and America, but if there's one thing that's blocking any change in the Middle East it's the fact that the old are in charge. It's the young who are paying the price for their failure to produce new ideas. It's young women and men who are blowing themselves up, young women, men and children who are being destroyed in the blast. As long as experience rules this will go on.

Both sides of course believe in God and both sides believe that God has a memory. God is terribly old of course, the ancient of days, and God apparently remembers everything. Your act of terror. My loss and bereavement. But it seems that even God's memory gets wiped from time to time. I looked up the Ten Commandments recently and discovered that God does indeed promise to punish human sin. But punishment is not eternal. God only exacts retribution for sin to the third and fourth generation. After that the slate is clean and we all start again. You might think that's bad enough? Why should great-grandchildren suffer for my mistakes? But experience suggests they often do. However, the last word is not with experience. Later in the Bible God produces a milder rule of retribution: everyone is accountable for their own mistakes; sin and retribution must not be passed on from generation to generation.

But in the Middle East the old are wiser than God. They know the situation is intractable and believe they can blast their way to security. Arabs and Israelis believe this too. Why then do the scriptures speak so often of a new birth, of a chosen king, of a child who will lead the wild animals to peace and make an end to war? Perhaps it is not an accident that one of the deadlocked spaces in the current conflict is the Church of the Nativity in Bethlehem. It's almost a symbol of spiritual impotence. Nothing can happen there at the moment – because the rule of the old ensures that the birth of peace is strangled.

ST GEORGE
THE PALESTINIAN

23 April 2002

He was probably a soldier in the service of the empire. Because he belonged to a religious minority, he was always a bit suspect. He came a cropper when a ruthlessly competent emperor decided to promote a cult of the state. Everyone was expected to conform, the one thing *he* couldn't do. He was taken into custody, stripped of his rank, tortured, tried and killed. Within a few years of his death a new emperor, to everyone's amazement, began to promote the very faith for which he had died.

And so he began a post-mortem career as a Christian saint and martyr. Today is St George's day, George the patron saint of the English. His flag, the English bit of the Union flag of Great Britain, will be fluttering today from churches and cathedrals. Recently our attention has been on St George's Chapel, Windsor, on St George as the patron of the Order of the Garter. He lives in the English imagination as he became in medieval legend, a heavily armoured knight charging at a green dragon.

This version of St George produces mixed feelings in our increasingly polarized society. It is easy for him to become a figurehead of a kind of fervent English nationalism that would have been very foreign to him. It's important to remember that the real George had nothing to do with Western Europe at all, let alone with the English part of these islands. He was probably Palestinian. He was adopted as one of the greatest of the martyrs by Christians of the East. Even today he doesn't belong to the English alone. We share him with Orthodox Greece.

I think that the real George has unexplored potential as a national figurehead. He is, after all, a foreigner, and reminds us of how the English have never been a pure race – our life and our language have always been enriched and changed by successive migrations. Then he is a soldier. He stands for self-discipline and loyalty which have been important in our history and will be even more important if we are to have a future.

He served the state faithfully, but when it made being a Christian a crime, he accepted the role of a religious dissident. He could not turn his faith into something bland, he could not be silent in the face of imperial aggression. He refused to bow down to human power, but he put his trust in the living God and his hope in the resurrection.

George is important for us because he calls us to attend to values that are deeper than our national or even personal interest. The white background on his flag is like the future, open for us to make of a diverse society a hell of conflict or a real community; the red cross is a testimony to the cost of courage. So, today, George and all saints and martyrs, pray for us.

IMAGES

5 July 2002

It was an efficient execution. One sharp blow from a metal object and off came her head. The rest of her stayed upright, being of marble, not flesh. The neat suit, folded hands and handbag were left standing cool and headless against the blood-red background of the Guildhall Gallery.

The man who beheaded Margaret Thatcher's statue came armed with intent and a cricket bat, but his rage increased as he faced her image and he grabbed a metal pole to do the deed. His violent emotion suggests that he wasn't making a purely political statement. He said to the magistrate yesterday that the statue was 'an idol'. He wanted to destroy its very essence. So the first woman prime minister symbolically lost her head; it was, after all, her headship that was resented.

That makes me think of other occasions when public art has been defaced. The statue of Winston Churchill in Parliament Square was daubed with red paint in a May Day riot, and made to sprout an anarchic Mohican hairdo. The dignity of the wartime prime minister was destroyed and his head became a gargoyle, a sinister green man.

Violence against images is always about power. The statues of the great stare beyond us, high on their plinths seeing our future for good or evil. Most of us have no problem with this kind of public art, we can live with significant figures in paint and stone whether or not we agree with their values. But for some the image becomes an idol, it blocks out the light. They react to the statue or portrait as though it is an affront designed to rob them of their selfhood. Their violence is a form of magic, like a witch sticking pins into an effigy.

Violence against statues is oddly impotent. It may cause shocks or smiles but it doesn't help us to place significant people in our developing history, to get a grip on who they really were and who we have become because of them. We need to deal with Mrs Thatcher's legacy, and her statue in the members' lobby will help us to do so. In the same way it is important that the figure of Oliver Cromwell stands outside Parliament, even though we decided not to abolish the monarchy he tried to destroy. His moment in our past was a great moment; he left us questions which are still being answered. What I think happens is that as time passes our oppositions gradually transform into new possibilities. This is a healing process, and it is one I believe all societies need. It's part of a Christian view of history, that what happens in time really matters, the blessings must be passed on and the sins redeemed.

And the marble Mrs Thatcher must go back to its maker, as in the end we all do.

BROKEN HEARTS

12 July 2002

On Tuesday the Church of England's General Synod voted to lift the ban on remarrying divorced people in church. Yesterday I discussed this with my newsagent, a Muslim. 'If you have a rule,' he said, 'you can't just change it.' He pointed out that Islam was more tolerant about such matters, but he felt that Christians should stick to the rules of their own faith.

The rule against remarriage is in the Gospels. Jesus taught that when a man and woman marry, a bond is forged which can't be broken. One of the most solemn moments in the Wedding Service is when the priest echoes his teaching by announcing: 'Those whom God has joined let no one divide', or 'let no man put asunder' as it used to be in the old Prayer Book. So why a rethink now? Is the Church just giving in to lax moral standards? Or even smoothing the path for Charles and Camilla?

The experience of many parish priests is that most people don't just fail at marriage. They fail and desperately want to try again. The Church preaches forgiveness and the possibility of making a fresh start, so why not for the divorced? Are they the exceptions to the Christian message?

It was simply awful being divorced half a century ago. I remember as a child the horror with which I learned that my friend's mum was one of 'those women'. I expected her to be a real vamp in lipstick and gold, not the rather anxious, tired-looking woman who opened the door when I went to tea. I thought the taint might stick, I knew there were churches where the divorced were shamed by having to sit apart. I wouldn't want it to be like that today.

So I have to try to make sense of why Jesus took the hard line he did. And I think I'm coming to an answer. If I look at the whole of his teaching I see again and again that his chief concern is for the vulnerable. Divorce in his time was fine for men, but it was often dire for women who had no rights in the matter. Wasn't his firmness, then, in order to protect those who stood to lose everything?

And doesn't that leave the Church, if it is to use his teaching intelligently, asking who, today, are the victims of divorce? Who needs protection? At that point, whether you're hard line or permissive becomes irrelevant because every case will be different. The victim could be a child, it could be an abandoned partner; and it could be the partners themselves, who for a host of reasons simply can't make this marriage work.

But given time and a fresh start a new relationship might have a chance. Humans are creative and can change and learn. Allowing some divorced people to remarry in church is a far from tidy answer, but for those whose hearts have been broken with their promises, it could be a small mercy.

SOMETHING FOR NOTHING

19 July 2002

It all seemed such a good idea at the time. To stash that thousand quid into an ISA, to listen to the adviser who said don't pay off the mortgage, here's a good investment. And now. Never did I think I would be turning the financial pages like episodes in a soap opera. Black Monday, a rally on Wednesday, a surge yesterday, another plummet tomorrow. Are we in fact seeing the beginning of the end of Western capitalism?

It's all there in the small print. 'The value of your investment can go up and down'. There are no guarantees. We know it in theory and yet we feel betrayed. And the betrayal is worse because we now know that to keep people like us happy at least one huge American company lied about its profits, and many others may have done so. People in the know, like the President of the United States, have the chance to sell out in time, but we're just left mourning our losses.

Can things ever get better? We need to remember that capitalism was born in a social and religious revolution. The new enterprises of the sixteenth century were hungry for money. The Church was always suspicious of money lending, but it gradually came to accept it, as long as the risk was shared between borrower and lender. Risk-free investments (those are the kind we like) were condemned as immoral, because it simply is immoral to get something for nothing. The system depended on investor and entrepreneur trusting one another and sharing a common risk. The whole gamble was underwritten by a code of honesty. Each player was accountable to each other, and to God, the ultimate keeper of accounts. I'm sure there were liars and cheats, then as now, but the reason capitalism has worked as well as it has is that there have always been enough honest, frugal puritans in business who feared God even more than they feared ruin.

The great reformer John Calvin saw the world as a theatre where human drive and ingenuity produce new wonders for the glory of God. Capitalism has been astonishingly successful in generating wealth. But the dream's gone sour. Perhaps we need to begin by examining ourselves, for money is a spiritual issue. I think it's true that too many of us thought we could have something for nothing, that whatever happened in the real world the markets would always bounce back higher and higher. When companies fiddle their accounts and call their losses profits, they are feeding our illusion, giving us what we want. And now we've come down with a hard bump.

It would be lovely to conjure pennies from heaven, but the capitalist dream is not built by magic. Hard work, thrift, honesty, prudence, thoughtful risk and patience are the virtues of successful enterprise: they also happen to be the virtues of the kingdom of heaven.

BLACKMAIL

7 October 2002

'If you won't be the sort of leader I want then I'll cause no end of trouble.' We've heard rumblings from all over the Tory party from individuals determined to put pressure on party leader Iain Duncan Smith during the next few days. We've heard similar things from the evangelical Church Society who are meeting today to plan their next move against Rowan Williams, the new Archbishop of Canterbury, whose views on the Bible they disagree with.

People who use the 'If you . . . then I' kind of argument always know what's right, what the party needs or what the Church needs. On the domestic front they are the people who are quite clear about what their marriage needs, and if only their spouse had the good sense to see it *their* way all would be well. It would be a betrayal of principle not to argue their point, spineless not to insist on the rightness of their cause. So they graciously and lovingly seek clarification. All you have to do is to follow this policy, make this declaration, drop or adopt this particular idea. Whatever's wrong is your fault. You are the aggressive one, whose policies, beliefs, behaviours are splitting the party, dividing the church, breaking up the marriage.

Every now and then you get a sudden insight into this common form of emotional blackmail, for that's what it is. 'If you want us to lose the next election', 'If you want our marriage to end', 'If you really want to destroy the Church' – the strategy is to claim and indeed to believe that, far from making demands or being difficult, you've simply been forced into your position by the other's intransigence. In psychology this is called passive aggression. In theology it is called the sin of presumption – because you presume your own innocence rather than seeking the judgement of God.

It is in fact a thoroughly aggressive way in which to behave. It is attempting to force an issue by emotional violence. We don't always recognize the violence because we live in a society where manipulation to get your way is often preferred to painstaking negotiation. As our society moves further away from the Christian values of self-restraint and respect for others I fear we will have to put up with more and more of these tantrums in public life.

Speaking of tantrums reminds me of the terrible threats of Violet Elizabeth Bott in the *William* books. Violet Elizabeth Bott was a very properly brought-up little girl. But when she didn't get her own way she had an unfailing weapon. She would cry: 'I'll thkweam and thkweam and thkweam until I'm thick. I can, you know.' I don't think she ever was actually sick, but everyone was so terrified that she might be that they rushed to placate her. Presumption is a sin that comes from weakness, from a failure to deal with reality. The answer is not to placate it but to stand up to it and make it show its true face.

BALI

14 October 2002

We all guessed there would be more terrorist violence, and now it's happened and once again it seems the killers have the advantage of unpredictability. Who would have thought of bombing Bali, a holidaymakers' Paradise?

I don't know about you, but my instinctive reaction to the news from Bali was to try to get my mind round it. What makes people do these wicked deeds? Why there and not elsewhere? I find myself trying to understand the bombers, and even wondering what it would be like to be fascinated at the pictures of the evil success I had achieved. Then I find myself asking, 'What do *they* really want? Is there anything I can do about it? Am I in some way part of what is to blame?' I think I am coming to see that these are the wrong questions. Wickedness of the kind we saw on Saturday night is a spiral movement downwards away from humanity, away from wisdom, away from any kind of connectedness or conversation. It flies in the face of a God of justice and mercy. When we try to understand it we have a hurdle to get over. Terrorists do not want to be understood. If they are understood they lose some of their power because what they really want is to control us by fear.

We do, though, have one advantage in the war against terrorism. It may be the only one, but I think in the long term it is more important than anything. It's that we know what goodness is. I don't mean goodness in the sense that we are right or superior or just nice or anything like that. Niceness gets us nowhere. I mean goodness in the everyday sense of what makes for human well-being. To be a terrorist you have to erase anything you know about your kinship with other human beings. These terrorists had to forget they knew anything about the goodness of families and holidays and work and leisure and ordinary human living. To do this they had to perform a spiritual lobotomy on themselves. Only so could they become the dark angels of terror, faceless agents of their cause.

I take comfort in times of terror from the Gospel of John which speaks of the light of God as something eternal, *the light that lightens everyone*. God's gift of conscience has not been taken away from human beings, though it is obscured for a while in the dust and wreckage of lives. 'The light shines on in the darkness', John says, 'and the darkness has never overcome it.' The Greek word for 'overcome' can also mean comprehend. The forces of darkness, all too human as they are, literally do not understand the goodness they seek to destroy. They don't get it. They can't see it. That is why they are terrifying, but it is also why the light will triumph in the end.

ADOPTION

21 October 2002

The new Adoption Bill was defeated in the Lords last week and it's unlikely to get through unscathed when it returns to the House of Commons in a couple of weeks' time. This is the bill that lets unmarried couples, including gay couples, adopt children. Those who opposed the bill predictably claimed to be protecting family values and the sanctity of marriage.

I find myself in a dilemma on this issue. The weakening of marriage is a real threat to society and yet when it comes to children who need parents the fact is that there are not nearly enough married people to go round. Stable married couples tend to get the pick of needy children. Those with more difficult backgrounds are often left languishing.

There are thousands of children in council homes waiting to be adopted. If they get to sixteen without finding parents they'll be out and on their own with no home to go back to, no good memories of family life to sustain them. If you ask these unwanted children what they dream of it's always the same: a mum and a dad and a home. It's impossible to match the dream exactly for everyone but the bill did try to make part of the dream come true.

Children are incredibly adaptable and many make do on heartbreakingly little, managing to glean love and self-esteem from less than ideal parents. This was well understood in the ancient world where adoption was more often seen as an honour than a second best. To be a chosen child meant acceptance, not rejection. It often strengthened family ties rather than threatened them. In our insecure times we are learning that children can thrive in all sorts of makeshift conditions. Where there is love and affection, where they are special, most children flourish.

Children know what they need and we should listen to them while they are able to tell us about their dreams. Jesus had harsh things to say about those who make little ones stumble. Too many of our children are stumbling because they haven't got parents, and end up on the streets or in prison. To know you are unwanted gets to the core of your identity; you cannot forget your shame, your sense of being rubbish in society's eyes. No one wanted you, so you are of no value, even to yourself.

And that's where I find the attempts to destroy this bill so heartless. In the name of family values it sets out to prevent the forming of families. No one is denying that married couples make the best parents, but it's a poor moral principle that makes the best the enemy of the good. We are in danger of saying to the neediest and most vulnerable children in society that if they can't have the best they can't have anything at all. And that is hypocrisy as well as heartlessness.

COLUMBIA DISASTER

3 February 2003

When President Bush comforted his fellow Americans on Saturday after the space shuttle tragedy he quoted from the fortieth chapter of Isaiah, where the ancient prophet of Israel is trying to comfort his troubled people. He tells them to look up to the heavens and he describes the creator calling the stars out by name, one by one, rather as a shepherd might call his sheep. The President said we could pray that the crew of *Columbia*, though they had not made it back to earth, had made it home.

The President gave us a picture of intimacy between the creator and the creation, between God and the souls of the seven brave individuals we saw on the front of our morning papers. This sense of intimacy does not just belong to the pages of the Bible; it is implicit in the science of our time. It is part of the sense of mystery which drives people to explore space, to spend years on painstaking research and to risk their lives to extend the boundaries of knowledge. Rick Husband, the commander, tried four times to become an astronaut. His childhood dream was to go to the stars. The fascination of science is that it unfolds the universe to us and shows us that we are not aliens here, but part of the whole space–time environment, our very bodies are made of elements that were first forged in the hot centres of dying stars. The mission of space shuttle *Columbia* was not showy. There were no celebrities, no passengers. The crew were there to do a job and wanted knowledge, not fame. We would never even have known their names and faces if all had gone well. As it was, most of us had heard the news within hours, and some within seconds. There could be no cover-up of this most intimate disaster, no hiding from the shock of it. It happened live and in our homes.

And of course we feel sorrow at the loss of life and the grief of the American people. But I am aware in myself of another less expected feeling, which is a kind of awe. The seven were in awe of the universe and loved what they did. Like other space travellers they were deeply moved by the sight of the earth floating below them. It was Colonel Ramon, the Israeli who had bombed an Iraqi reactor in 1982, who said, 'The earth looks marvellous from up here, so peaceful, so wonderful and so fragile', and then he added, thinking of his troubled country, 'All of us down there have to keep it clean and good.' In times like this we really do have a chance to stand back and share that vision, to recognize that the oneness of our world is a greater truth than its divisions, and that the intimacy we share by being part of this astonishing universe is even deeper than our hatreds.

FREEDOM

24 April 2003

The sight of blood-soaked pilgrims on their way to the holy city of Karbala has alarmed those hoping for a peaceful transition to democracy in Iraq. One report suggested that we should take the outburst of religious fervour at face value, as though it was what might have happened in a Christian country if a tyrannical state had banned the observance of Good Friday for forty years. But others saw something more sinister going on, the stirrings of a religious revolution, like that in Iran when the Shah was deposed.

I think the pictures of the seething, chanting worshippers make us face the awful paradox of Western democracy which is this: supposing a free people freely and democratically choose not the kind of liberal government that we presume democracy entails, but theocracy, government by God? Supposing in a free and fair election the majority do actually vote for God? It's not impossible. It's already clear that not everyone in the world sees Coca-Cola and short skirts as the longed-for fruits of freedom. Why should we imagine that everyone wants to be our sort of democrat? It's an immediate question as we think about Iraq, but it's also a question as we reflect on the situation throughout the Middle East. An earlier generation of Muslim reformers was indeed composed of democrats who supported Western ideals of government, but now millions of Muslims believe Western democracy is as hopelessly corrupt as the tyrannies they live under today. So why should they not freely choose a God of justice and order?

Before we faint with horror, it's worth reminding ourselves of English history. Oliver Cromwell's statue stands in Parliament Square. He was the founder of our parliamentary democracy. He brought to an end the absolute rule of kings. But he was no secular democrat in our modern sense. He was a genuine warrior for God, who was prepared to fight with the Bible in one hand

and a sword in the other. He did not want a pluralistic state but a Protestant and Christian one ordered on principles he believed were derived from the Word of God itself. The result was civil war and our one and only theocratic government. It was only after Cromwell's death and the restoration of a restricted monarchy that anything resembling our liberal, free society began to emerge. Our slow transition from tyranny has produced stability and tolerance. The coalition governments say they want to create such a society in Iraq. But freedom is freedom. You can't prescribe what it might contain for someone else without restricting it. When the people of Israel in the Bible chose kings rather than rule by judges, God groaned for them, seeing the oppression that kings would bring. But freedom cannot overrule even in the interests of freedom. That is the unnerving paradox which we can't quite bring ourselves to face.

ASCENSION DAY

28 May 2003

Today is a Christian festival, Ascension Day – but it's one which often gets ignored because it doesn't come with a holiday attached. You used to be able to get a day off school if you could persuade your parents to write to the head saying you had to go to church. I could never decide whether it was worth the risk of incurring a reputation for piety, and I suspect my mother would never have agreed to be part of the plot. Still, we sang a rousing hymn at morning assembly about Jesus Christ ascending into heaven and sensed something good about the approach of summer and something bad about the approach of exams. It was a small pause, a reminder that there is more going on than the particular preoccupations of today reveal.

Sacred time is hard to come by these days, and we've grown unaccustomed to its rhythms. We feel that if religion is to exist at all today it must be relevant and useful. Such a lot of Christian talk is about God's concern for the world, God's involvement with the world, God's pain at the pain of the world, where was God in Iraq, etc. – as though God's internal life were driven by our news agenda.

Yet the Ascension is about Jesus Christ leaving this world. It is the opposite of Christmas, when we say God came among us; now he's going away. There are some marvellously comic depictions of the event. There's a church in Jerusalem which treasures the impressions of two bare feet in a bit of exposed rock in its courtyard as though it were the authentic divine lift-off pad. And there are plenty of feet disappearing into clouds in medieval and renaissance art.

This comedy should point us to the fact that the Ascension is about perspective, about realizing that God sees the world not just in agonized close-up but from a lens as long as eternity. God's point of view is not ours, and that's actually a good thing for us because it means he's free from our agendas and so he cannot be manipulated or controlled by us.

Religion can do nothing for us if it doesn't save us from ourselves. If God is too intimate, too wound up with my story, our needs, my people's suffering, our rights and your responsibilities, then religious allegiance becomes no more than disguised egoism – a badge, like tribe or race, to defend ourselves with and batter away at others who are different. This is the tragic role of religion in our world and it does us no good at all.

The hymns of Ascensiontide speak of Christ conquering death and sin. They are almost irresponsibly cheerful, as though from God's point of view the sin and the misery we inflict on one another are not the last word. There is something more important than the news agenda – and that is the Good News.

OUR FACES

4 June 2003

Cindy Sherman is the elusive celebrity who has made a career of photographing her own face in hundreds of different guises. An exhibition of her work has just opened at the Serpentine Gallery. When she was an art student she had learnt the conventions of drawing and painting. But she was dissatisfied with her efforts and is quoted as asking, 'Why do I spend my time copying things . . . ?' That's when she started experimenting with her own face, dressing up in countless costumes and disguises. When I first heard about it I was appalled. I wanted to write this off as pure narcissism, the 'me' generation run riot, idolatrously in love with itself because it has dethroned God and despised beauty, truth and goodness. But then I saw some of the pictures and my view began to change.

Go into the Serpentine Gallery and you'll see her as a grotesque clown, or doubling up for an Old Master, as a porn idol, or a killer, or the Virgin Mary. No two portraits are alike. These photographic snippets are a collage of human life. Some of them look wholly authentic, others are deliberately faked so you can see the artifice, the false lighting, the imperfect make-up. The message seemed to be, we create ourselves as works of art, mannequins. I began to find a sadness in it all. Weren't these images a terrible commentary on our inner emptiness, on the fact that we all play bit parts in our lives – that we are all fragmented, clown and artist, victim and criminal? Because we no longer believe in God we no longer believe in ourselves. No image can be trusted. We are hollow, soulless beings in an empty universe of shadows.

But then I read an art critic who had seen something else in Cindy Sherman's work and reacted not with anger or sadness but with excitement and recognition. What these pictures show, this critic said, is that we are not all different. In spite of our masks and pretences, in spite of what others to do us and we do to ourselves there is a consistency in human nature. It is the same eyes that look out on the world. The truth is not that we are all irreconcilably different, but that we are all the same. I go back to Cindy Sherman's frustrated remark when she was an art student, 'Why do I spend my time copying things . . . ?' What she has done in her thirty years of self-portrayal is discover the freshness of the human face. It's her own face but it is also all our faces. For we are not just isolated individuals, nor are we disguises and part-selves. Plato thought it first and then it comes into the Bible. Humanity is made in the image of God, and that is not only where our true identity lies but it is also the hope of the world.

DAVID KELLY AND THE TRUTH ABOUT WMD

21 July 2003

What is truth? It is a question for all of us this morning as we reflect on David Kelly's lonely death on Friday. We talk so much about truth, and yet we understand it very little. We try to live as if there is simply truth and lies. But that itself is, forgive me, a pious untruth, because the truth I see is always limited. There is a whacking great plank in my eye, as Jesus once rather rudely said, and it runs right through my line of sight. It is my prejudices, my delusions and my fears. But the really interesting thing is, I don't see the plank in *my* eyes, I see it in yours: in what you unconsciously add to what I say to you, or what you screen out as irrelevant. What is truth? Pontius Pilate asked Jesus that question but he did not wait for an answer. If he had, things might have turned out differently.

Perhaps the best we can hope for is to acquire a kind of nose for truth, for the feel of it, the taste of it, in all its complexity. When we believed God knew the truth, it let us off the hook a bit. We didn't have to know it all. We didn't have to be right. We could be less anxious, less self-protective. It also left us open to judgement. We could rest our case in God's hands even if we lost, because we knew that in the end, the truth would shine out. Even our suspicions would lead us to the truth. There might, in the mercy of God, be space for apologies, for forgiveness.

The inquiry into David Kelly's death will proceed by asking questions. Careful questions, *yes or no* questions, *who said what to whom and when* questions. It will try to trace the gaps and elaborations, the little significant slippages that happen when individuals don't wholly understand what they are being told, the omissions that creep in to protect a bigger truth or a darker lie, the mistakes that occur when we think we already know the truth and are merely looking for confirmation of what we already know. We will come out at the end of it with some kind of picture, some way of distributing the blame among the already known suspects and perhaps others whose role has not yet come to light.

A death like this shows us the price of our perpetual duplicity. It is a time for self-searching and for the ancient virtue of humility. Truth is not easy for humankind, but as we commend David Kelly to his creator, we can ask that God will take this tangled tale and unwind it thread by thread until the truth shall make us free.

YOM KIPPUR

6 October 2003

It is thirty years since the outbreak of the Yom Kippur war, and the aggressions of that war are still around, as in the weekend bombing in Haifa and the Israeli strike on Syria. It's easy for us to wring our hands *yet again* over other people's violence, but the spirit of Yom Kippur asks something more of us. It is the Day of Atonement. The mood is one of penitence. It is one of the spiritual insights of Judaism that before we can greet the future, we must repent of our past sins.

We British have some of our own sins to examine in the long history of this particular conflict. This was once explained to me by a priest living in the Holy Land who said that all the problems came from the fact that the British had promised the same land to both Jews and Palestinians. An over-simplification no doubt, but it sums up at least part of what British Middle Eastern diplomacy was about in the middle years of the last century. To placate both sides just enough – and to upset both sides just enough – to keep our national interests intact. Not a huge sin you might think; you might even say it contained a streak of British common sense.

But today it makes me squirm. Behind such double-edged diplomacy is a very British assumption that our history and experience has given us a unique ability to understand both sides of every conflict. We alone have the balanced view. It's a convenient assumption because it enables us to keep on reasonably good terms with everyone, while making promises we never quite manage to keep. Hypocrisy is part of our national character and it is expressed in our political and religious life. I know it from the inside as British and English and as a minister of our national Church with its attractive but rather implausible claim to have something to offer to absolutely everyone. It may not surprise you to know that there are two Anglican churches within a mile of one another in Jerusalem: Christ Church which is evangelical, missionary minded, and generally friendly to Israel, and St George's Cathedral, which is catholic, concerned with social justice and tends to support the Palestinians. We do so like to have it both ways. And though balanced diplomacy can be a virtue, it has led us into some unhelpful delusions, in particular the almost biblical delusion that we British really are rather special in the world, a nation of nations, not like other nations. The fact is that we do not know where peace lies and it is often well-meaning interference from outside which makes peace impossible.

If the nations stoking the fires of this conflict stopped trying to make peace, perhaps Jew and Arab, Israeli and Palestinian could find it for themselves.

SEXUAL ANXIETY

13 October 2003

Tonight Channel 4 starts screening its adult version of *Teenage Big Brother* with its brief, real-life sex scene. The fumblings of Tommy and Jade along with their discussions of religion and politics have been rescheduled at peak time.

Of course sex used to be a private matter. We did it, or abstained, but either way we didn't talk about it much. We accepted that sex was a strong force in human affairs, and our religious codes told us that we needed to civilize our desires and make them human. In the Marriage Service the Prayer Book didn't romanticize sex but warned us sternly against behaving like brute beasts. Those who married should approach their partners reverently, discreetly, advisedly, soberly and in the fear of God. Such an approach did little to assuage our curiosity.

Everyone had to find out about sex for themselves. It meant that sex remained fascinating, but was also deeply embarrassing. The potent combination of lust and shame actually protected us and let us take our most intimate risks in private.

But today, thanks to the media, the Church, footballers and celebrities we have all learnt to be open, frank and explicit. We know everything there is to know. And yet, bizarre though it seems, our curiosity still isn't satisfied. In fact the more we talk about it, the more baffled, shamed and curious we seem to become. We measure our own level of sexual contentment not by what we do or don't do, but by comparing ourselves with other people. So there's plenty of room for envy, aggression and heartbreak. Sex has become a vicarious activity, like football in an unfit society. This is telling because alongside the endless need to know about other people's sex lives, the media tell another story. There is, it appears, a widespread epidemic of sexual disappointment. Tiredness, boredom and overkill have taken their toll in the bedroom.

The rush to show these poor kids on *Big Brother* speaks to me not of frankness or fun, but of something much sadder; the desperate anxiety that there is in our adult world. This is no doubt why the television executives want to push this episode and even why they claim it has educational value. They know we are really worried about ourselves. We want to know whether we are getting enough sex and whether we are doing it right. We no longer know how to trust to nature, intimate dialogue and real feeling. We no longer know how to be shy. Perhaps Tommy and Jade can restore our innocence, our belief that sex can mean something.

I think it is rather tragic that adults have to spy on teenagers to reassure themselves that sex is worth while.

CONFRONT THE YOB WITHIN

24 October 2003

Graffiti, casual theft, foul language, car crime, sick in the streets. The recent shop-a-yob campaign sponsored by the *Sun* is one symptom of a growing revolt against anti-social behaviour. There's a weighty bill steamrollering through the House of Lords designed to crack down on the sixty thousand recorded acts of anti-social behaviour which occur each day. The proposed legislation means that the police can be called in if two or three people believe that something unpleasant is going on, which could be almost anything which looks, note, *looks*, intimidating or aggressive.

The bill seems designed to arouse the law-abiding majority to hit back. Nip bad behaviour in the bud, suspicion is ground enough to get you shopped. It's the revenge of the privet hedge. But it worries me because, just like the bad behaviour it's meant to prevent, it depends on feelings and fears. It's part of the shallow emotionalism that runs through our whole society. We've gone along too easily with the pop psychology that tells us that any expression of feeling is justified as long as it is sincere. So when people get angry, or feel frustrated, they feel it's all right to swear or threaten obscenely. In fact it's almost shameful not to. You've got to keep your self-respect after all. And if you don't respect yourself, no one else will. So we are being wound up to be more suspicious of one another, more fearful, more ready to take offence. We've forgotten the lesson of the nursery that giving expression too easily to rage can make everyone hate you; once you start taking offence, the whole world seems to be insulting you.

I'm not suggesting we don't have a problem, but we're in danger of making it worse. A civilized society trains people to understand emotion, rather than simply to emote. Religion helps us to see our behaviour as through the eyes of God. We are accountable, we will be judged. After the Reformation it became fashionable for parish churches to have the Ten Commandments inscribed on their east walls so that the worshippers had to look at them while they prayed. The Commandments used to be recited by the priest at the beginning of every Communion Service. I once thought this was awful and legalistic and opposed to the Christian ethic of love. But as society has reduced love to mere sentimentality I find I've changed my mind. Dry, laconic, boring; the famous 'Thou shalt nots' could never be described as exciting but they do prohibit us from wrecking other people's lives. No one can get emotional about the Ten Commandments, and that's exactly why they're useful. They remind us of the need for restraint over our emotions: because murder, theft, adultery, defamation and covetousness all begin with emotions which get out of control. It's one thing to shop yobs, but it might be much better to confront the yob within.

NEW YEAR HONOURS

31 December 2003

The row over the honours system has taken some of the shine off today's New Year List. I woke up wondering whether the papers would be blank, or full of refusals of honours that are now apparently tainted. But no, it seems there are still enough individuals who are pleased to be recognized publicly, bringing pleasure and pride to their friends and families.

I'm interested in those who say no. I can understand why you might if you felt you were genuinely undeserving. The detective writer Dorothy L. Sayers refused to accept an honorary degree from the Church because she felt her private life disqualified her – she had an illegitimate child. But most of those who turn down honours today do so because they believe the system is corrupt, or they don't want to be associated with royalty, with patronage, with 'Buggins' turn', with a vanished empire, with the whole seedy establishment package. In other words, for these refuseniks, the honour isn't good enough.

I'm not entirely convinced by all this. It's nonsense to assume that any system of public honours could be conducted with the complete openness and transparency that some have advocated. Think of the embarrassment of being nominated and rejected in public, of aggressive lobbying and counter lobbying, of getting your friends to argue you up from MBE to OBE. The secret conversations revealed in the *Sunday Times* are remarkable for being so ordinary, showing so much that goes on when people have to select some and not others for public recognition. Refusal of an honour may appear principled, but it may also be a form of inverted snobbery. There are those among the great and the good who don't like being the object of others' opinion, who are affronted at the very thought of having their merits debated, by, of all boring people, civil servants. Stardom today depends on having control of your own publicity.

One of the distinctive virtues of the Christian faith is humility. That does not mean running yourself down or pretending you're worthless. On the contrary, it means accepting that others have a right to a view of you which may be lower or higher than your own. So I am not sure whether to admire those who turn down honours or whether they are in fact displaying a kind of arrogance, which in the end devalues the contribution of the lesser known and truly humble, who may have slogged away for years without expecting anything. After all, the stars are there to pepper the list with a bit of glamour, a brutal fact which our sportsmen, at least, seem to have accepted with grace. Can a star find humility? Christmas ends in the wise men coming to the stable of Jesus and laying down their treasures. Perhaps such humility is beyond our reach, but it's sad that some of our stars are too self-important to share the same gong as a dinner lady.

CREDIT-CARD BILL

8 January 2004

Any day now I'm expecting my credit-card bill for December. We've probably all spent a lot this Christmas – and most of us didn't stop when Christmas was over. The sales drew us out to spend again, using up more credit. It's a funny word, 'credit'. It suggests something free, a prize, a gift. But of course it's actually the opposite. Credit is debit, debt. Having credit makes us feel in charge, our plastic cards close the gap between desire and possession. It feels like a bargain, an exercise of personal choice to which we all feel entitled. But today's choice is tomorrow's restriction, because debt is not a never-never land. It is an obligation for almost all of us; and for some, an ever-tightening prison that ends in the terror of loan sharks and bailiffs.

But at a lower level everyone's in debt, even the Chancellor of the Exchequer borrows on our behalf. And even his borrowings have to be paid for. Those virtuous debts, mortgages on property, actually tie us up for years. Whatever dreams I might have had of doing something really imaginative or risky with my life are buried in the bricks and mortar of my so-called investment. It's likely that alongside their mortgages, university students will soon be carrying new long-term debts, paying back the cost of their courses. And then they'll have to get jobs that pay them enough to service their debts. There are lots of people who feel a longing to do something that they can't afford to do, which may be to enter a fulfilling but low-paid caring profession, or to go abroad as a volunteer, or to enter the ministry of the Church. What holds them back is not selfishness or doubt but the mortgage, the credit-card bills, the need to maintain a steady income which pays off what they owe. We are slaves to our salaries, which bring us not freedom but a form of bondage which enchains the human heart. Perhaps it is not surprising that in the Bible, debt is the deepest form of slavery which takes away the essential freedom to serve God with all our heart and soul and mind and strength. Sometimes I wonder whether the angers and frustration and addictions of our society are not a symptom that we are chafing in our chains. It was certainly true for me that it was only when offered redundancy that I could afford to let go of my securities and respond to the call of the gospel. And then I knew, as Charles Wesley knew, what it is to be released from debt: 'My chains fell off, my heart was free, I rose, went forth and followed thee.'

EVIL'S SELF-DEFEAT

15 January 2004

Last weekend I watched *The Lord of the Rings*: one of the great epic fantasies of our age, with its long-drawn-out drama of the clash between good and evil.

Its author, Tolkien, realized, as many fantasy writers do, that evil is essentially empty and lifeless. Evil is the eye of Sauron that sees while remaining unseen. Evil is the dark riders with no faces beneath their cloaks. Our newspapers have been full of the now familiar face of Harold Shipman, the murderous doctor who has been found dead in his prison cell. There is a sense of deep frustration that he has for a final time escaped scrutiny, by controlling his exit from this life. The relatives of the people he killed feel cheated. One of them said yesterday that he had always harboured the desire to meet him face to face just to ask him 'Why?' But real evil doesn't know the answer why. Shipman denied his guilt and no one was able to find a motive for his killings. Beneath his bland, even kindly face there was, it seems, a blank. Our minds rebel against this. We look for reasons – in childhood, in temperament, in the desire for financial gain, in a bid to secure a pension for his wife. We get psychologists to profile him, we ask his teachers, his patients and his poor sad wife. We stare at the face of the papers as we stared at the face of Myra Hindley and Fred West, trying to find the face behind the face, the real person within. But none of them could ever really tell us why they did what they did. I wonder if Tolkien's instinct isn't right and that the reason we can't find a reason is that there isn't one. The evil heart is a black hole which absorbs everything and gives nothing out.

St Augustine once described evil as the 'absence of good'. It sounds like a rather weak description but I think that was the point he was trying to make. God is good, and so is all that God has made. Evil is when a person realizes that by murder or lying or apathy they can unravel creation, and thus take revenge on God for disturbing the darkness of non-existence. The last thing evil can do is to unravel itself, which is why there is a kind of weird justice in Shipman's sordid death. He has taken himself out of our world. Of course this enrages us. We would rather have hell and the devil and the fires of judgement because at least then there would be something to relate to, to engage with, to inter-rogate. The triumph of evil, then? No, a challenge, but rather its impotence and self-defeat. Having failed to be great it simply tidies itself away and de-creates itself. And life goes on.

SPERM

22 January 2004

Hearty, rugger-playing medical students used to do it for cash. Concerned married men did it out of altruism. Sperm donation has made it possible for some childless couples to have families. But now the anonymity which sperm donors have had guaran-teed is clashing with what many believe is the right of every child to know who its biological parents are.

Two rights are on a collision course with one another. But underneath the clash there is a question about personal identity. Do you need to know who your biological father is to know who you really are? Well, perhaps, when it comes to inherited diseases. To deny my genetic inheritance is to live as though my true self is somehow detached from my physical nature and the things that happen to me. That view sounds profound, but I think it's actually an escape, and one to which religious people are particularly prone. But there's an opposite view which falls into the same error. This is that I simply *am* the product of my genes, defined by the material reality created in the instant fusion of a particular sperm and egg.

So if I don't know the origin of the sperm that went into my conception, I am carrying around an alien presence, a hidden father who keeps his secrets and therefore denies me the emotional truth of my being. This looks plausible. It *is* different to grow up knowing that the person you call father is not your biological father, but to make too much of it seems misguided to me. It can also be a kind of escape, a longing for a fantasy father. I'm not convinced that there is such a thing as an essential self. The person that I am has grown from my conception out of a million possibilities, as a result of the choices and chances that life has brought me. *Who I am* is what I do with my genetic blueprint, and is worked out day by day in relationship to others – to the parents who brought me up, to siblings, to the wider world, and, I would want to say, to God. The Christian faith addresses God as Father, not least to remind us that we are not merely the end-product of biological events. Life is a process of transformation that continues beyond death, and includes – but does not stop at – the death and disintegration of my body. We bear the image of the man of dust, says St Paul, but we will bear the image of Christ, the image of glory. If this insight is true then it is wrong for me to identify myself with either my physical genes or any kind of spiritual essence; either the dust or glory. It is on the way from dust to glory that I become who I am.

HUSSAM ABDU

26 March 2004

The tormented face of Hussam Muhammed Abdu stared out from the front pages yesterday. This boy – reported to be only fourteen – had apparently been given a cash prize of £14 to go to an Israeli checkpoint wearing a vest full of explosives and blow himself up. He appeared like a confused penguin, in a huge army jacket with sleeves that reached to his knees. If he'd succeeded in his ghastly mission he would have been the thirtieth under-age suicide bomber to have perished in the intifada. But as he approached the checkpoint he lost his nerve and burst into tears. He simply didn't want to die. It's a tragi-comic story – which the Israelis describe as an example of Palestinian cruelty towards their own children. At the same time his friends are disowning him, claiming that he was always a bit dim and couldn't possibly have known what he was doing.

When I heard it reported yesterday I was reminded of another story from the beginning of the third century, when Christians all over the Roman Empire risked persecution for their faith. When the father of a devout Egyptian family was executed for being a Christian, his son was determined to follow him to martyrdom. He was just about to set off to give himself up when he found that his mother had hidden all his clothes, judging, as his biographer put it, 'that modesty would get the better of his courage'. I've always been amused by the thought of that naked young man hunting around for his tunic to go and get killed in. His mother's action, though, had more lasting consequences than even she could have guessed. The boy, whose name was Origen, grew up to be one of the greatest Bible scholars and philosophers the Christian Church has ever had. He did far more for his fellow Christians by defending the faith against state paganism than he would have done by dying prematurely. I wish there were more Origens among the Muslims, Jews and

Christians striving for survival in the Middle East. People who, even in desperate times, learnt to think about the Lord God and the requirements he makes of us rather than about getting advantages over their enemies.

It takes a kind of grim courage to be a martyr. It also takes courage to stay alive. Hussam Abdu is reported to have said that he tried to blow himself up because he didn't feel loved. His low sense of self was casually exploited by those who set him up to die, drumming it into him that he would be a hero in heaven. In the end, pathetic though his gesture was, he made the most important choice he could have made – which was not to seek worth as defined by others, but to stay alive. Whatever the outcome of his life, his gesture challenges us all – Israelis, Palestinians and us by-standers. In that way his living was more important than his death could ever have been.

DIVORCE

24 April 2004

When I was growing up in the 1950s divorce was a shocking misfortune which happened to almost nobody I knew. Today, of course, it's everywhere, but our divorce laws are still strangely out of step with the rest of our lives. The law still assumes that women are inferior to men. This used to mean women were punished by divorce, it now means that they are treated as victims who need special protection. So the custody rules favour women, and so often do financial settlements, especially for celebrities. Karen Parlour, who has a quarter of a million a year in maintenance, is suing her footballer ex-husband for 37.7 per cent of his future earnings. Her lawyers are claiming that she deserves the extra because for the fourteen years of their marriage she looked after the home and saved him from drinking too much. This will be a test case. If she wins there'll be a stream of other claims on the future earnings of men.

The book of Genesis speaks of men and women being in the image and likeness of God. If you read the text carefully you see that the divine image is not in the individuals but in the relationship they share. Marriage makes people more like God. I wonder if that is why, when a marriage breaks up, it's as though the demons are let loose. Adam and Eve replay the Fall. In the emotional aftermath men often appear at their most aggressive and women at their most manipulative. I find it simply sordid that the emotional support given in a marriage could be treated in future as a mere asset, to be paid back in hard cash.

A better way would be to see what can be retrieved of the broken image, and whether some kind of dignity and trust can be rebuilt. This is the challenge for ministers, counsellors, even divorce lawyers. The end of a marriage should involve a just division of the assets of the marriage, without tying up the future; and shared responsibility for children, not a possessive grab for control of them. It's only in our sob, sob 'I have suffered so much' culture that emotional arguments produce such rich rewards.

Our marriage traditions have something to answer for here. The summer magic of weddings leaves its hangover; we punish the failure of our dreams by meting out punishment and revenge. But if trust is important in marriage, trust needs to be part of a good divorce. With my upbringing, and the investment I have as a Christian minister in marriage and family life, I hesitate to put the words 'good' and 'divorce' together. But if we are to grow up about all this we must learn to do so. We need there to be such a thing as a good divorce. And the evidence suggests that we haven't got it yet.

WEEPING AND RENEWAL

17 May 2004

Today Maxine Carr, after serving her sentence for the part she played in obstructing the Soham murder case, begins her first week of freedom. I should say the person who *was* Maxine Carr, because, hidden from public view, we must assume that she'll be using a different name, her passport to a new life.

In the court of public opinion the figure of Maxine Carr has divided us, the jury. To some, she is an innocent victim; to others a wicked accomplice. In all this she has been robbed of her complexity. And that reminds me of an occasion when I was a documentary maker and was filming in the United States. The hired electrician who was setting the lights for an interview came up and asked me, as he no doubt routinely did, 'Are we lighting for or against?' Such questions reveal our moral superficiality. They show us that we can't deal with the fact that we are not simply good or evil, but a mixture.

We know *really* that Maxine Carr was neither a willing accomplice, nor was she wholly innocent; much has been made of her dodgy benefit claims. Small-scale stuff, perhaps, and yet not so far from the small, convenient half-truths many of us employ to make our lives a bit more comfortable. What she did not see, as we fail to, is that the habit of small lies blunts our moral edge, so when we have to smooth things over with a big lie, we are already well practised in the art and we slip over the edge – sometimes into real trouble – without even realizing we've done so.

Is she then particularly unfortunate that she has been exposed, that life has played a dirty trick on her? You could see it that way. But you could also see her story in the light of the Christian gospel. I always despair when the 'hate' brigade start talking about there being no forgiveness for people like her, and take a horrible pleasure in her distress. In the Christian moral tradition, all of us are sinners, in love with our own illusions. The

Christian gospel is a wake-up call to recognize the consequences of living untruthfully.

Sin opens the way to hell and judgement, precisely that kind of black and white judgement which we mete out so easily to characters like Carr. So I hope that prison to her was not only a place of doing her time, but of revelation – of weeping, yes, but of renewal too. Nothing will wipe away her memories of who she was and what she did, but the moral slate is clean now and the force of law is behind her as she tries to begin again. The Reformation saints said shockingly that the human condition was one of total depravity. But they also said that if we confessed our sins God is faithful and just to forgive us our sins and to cleanse us from all unrighteousness.

FOOD SINNERS

31 May 2004

The government's report on obesity has produced a rash of pictures of overweight children, as the litany of disease predictions piles up around them. Fat is the new sin; which is odd because only a couple of years ago the government was warning about anorexia, and scolding the fashion industry for promoting superthin models. Then I go to the supermarket and I see what the fuss is *really* all about. The frozen chips are all one size, so are the vine-ripened tomatoes, so are the slices of plastic ham, so are the baked beans. Even the potatoes are trying hard to measure up. One size is efficiency, neat packaging, easy transport, and, of course, I, the customer have been trained not only to like it but to depend on it. I know, you see, that twenty standard-size raspberries, half a banana, and one and half kiwi fruit provide three of my five portions of fruit and veg before I've even got on to the perfectly uniform florets of broccoli which soak up dangerous free radicals.

So perhaps what the government wants is for people to come in one size too. Think what a blessing it would be if they did. Think of the savings to the clothing industry; none of us would need scales any more, we would be blissfully standardized, from romper suits to coffins.

The problem is that those targeted as food sinners don't always respond well to the call for conformity. It's not unknown for the extremely fat to yo-yo into extreme thinness. Anyway being fat is hard enough to bear without being humiliated as well. When I was eight, and, well let's say, a sturdy little girl, a school doctor weighed me, tutted, lifted my vest and then poked her fingers into my tummy pointing out to the school nurse with disgust 'rolls of fat'. That turned me from a relatively cheerful if tubby child into a desperately self-conscious tubby pre-adolescent; if my temperament had been different I might have stopped eating altogether. It's not good for the soul to be the object of horrified fascination. But perhaps there is a spiritual answer to our anxieties about food.

The old habit of saying grace for what's on your plate at least made you think before you stuffed your face. Yesterday was Pentecost, the feast of the Holy Spirit. God's creation is fantastically diverse, the Spirit delights in variety. On the supermarket shelves are the cultivated wonders of the natural world and we are invited to discern what is good for us and delight in our food as God's gift. There is no standard human shape; our size, our life and probably our diseases and our eventual death are all written into our genes. If we worried less and gave thanks for every mouthful we would probably have a better chance of living out our natural span.